I have a hectic schedule. I have been involved in multiple c[...] and clubs as a way to feel important and worthy in other people's eyes. The D*I*V*A*S study took me through some thought provoking, self-examination exercises and made me realize that God has a specific purpose for my life. I now balance my schedule with God inspired activities and appointments! Sherri and Donna, thank you for teaching me how much God loves me and that He finds me worthy.

Tonya. C. ~ Director of Medical Facility/Mom

D*I*V*A*S showed me how to step out of my past and into God's wonderful and exciting plan for my life. This book is a must read for any woman who is ready for REAL JOY regardless of her circumstances.

Debbie M. ~ Wife/Mother/Grandmother

I have made a career out of helping others set and obtain healthy fitness goals. I can now say I have truly experienced success in my spiritual walk, personal relationships, and business by incorporating goal setting and God's plan into my day-to-day routine. Thanks D*I*V*A*S for helping me think of my life, business and spiritual walk in a whole new way – God's way!

Angela V. ~ Personal Fitness Trainer/ Business Owner

This program is one that has challenged, grown and ministered to me, like no other program I have experienced. It has given me the tools to become all the Lord has planned for me.

Debbie S. ~ Pastor's Wife

The D*I*V*A*S class was both fascinating and enlightening for me. Sherri and Donna's practical approach to accountability inspired me to make difficult changes in my life – but not to do it alone! I now have another sister in Christ to encourage, support, and help me stay focused on my spiritual disciplines.

Debbie C. ~ Office Manager

Are you searching for a fresh approach to accountability and spiritual growth in your life or your ministry? Then *D*I*V*A*S of the Divine* is the answer. Thanks Sherri and Donna for being God's vessel in creating this powerful resource. It will change many!

Anne B. ~ Director, Women of Carolina Conference

Carolina Baptist Association Women's Ministry Consultant

I can honestly say that *D*I*V*A*S of the Divine* changed my life! Over weeks of self-examination, prayer, and goal setting, I felt myself emerge from the depths I was falling to. This Bible study equipped me with tools that I will use for the rest of my life. For the first time in my life I know what God wants for me, and I'm setting goals to get there. I'm happier than I've ever been – in work, friendships, family, and with my husband. Thank you D*I*V*A*S! You saved my life….my heart….my soul, and for that I am eternally grateful.

Katie C. ~ Personal Trainer

Living a God-centered life full of joy seemed like a fairytale until I discovered *D*I*V*A*S of the Divine*. This study helped me take off my blinders, re-discover scriptural truth, and develop an intimate relationship with the Author of Joy.

Bridgette J. ~ Stay-at-Home Mom

D·I·V·A·S of the Divine

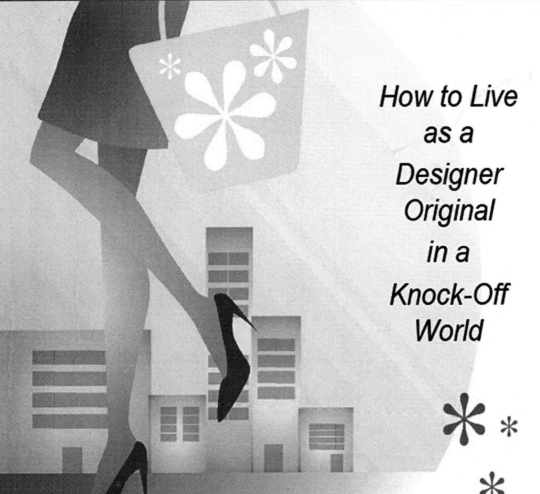

How to Live
as a
Designer
Original
in a
Knock-Off
World

Donna McCrary & Sherri Holbert

To order additional copies of this resource, visit www.hensleypublishing.com.

HENSLEY
PUBLISHING

Image Credit: Dreamstime.com, by Madartist

ISBN 10: 1-56322-108-X

ISBN 13: 978-156322-1088

D*I*V*A*S of the Divine: How to Live as a Designer Original in a Knock-Off World

About Photocopying This Book

Acknowledgements

Thank you to our Heavenly Father for allowing us the life experiences, education and inspiration to create the D*I*V*A*S life coaching study. We are extremely blessed and overwhelmed by the way God is using this unique curriculum in the lives of the many women who have already participated in it.

We want to thank our families, and ourLiving Water Baptist Church friends who have offered feedback, support, encouragement, and most importantly their prayers. We love each of you!

We give special thanks to our publishing mentor and dear friend, Linda Gilden. Your connections, advice, and inspiration have been invaluable to both of us. Thank you!

Thanks and appreciation to Carolyn Sisk (Sherri's Mom) for endless hours of proofing. Thank you, Mom, for always believing in me, encouraging me to live life with a positive attitude and to always give my best. I love you, Mom!

This project would not have been successful without the support, rational thoughts, words of wisdom, and endless hours of "editing" from our precious husbands, Rick and Jamie. Words cannot express what you mean to us. You have inspired us to seek God's path for our lives and have always believed in us. We love you.

TABLE OF CONTENTS

INTRODUCTION

Welcome ladies, to an exciting, life-changing adventure! God's promises of guidance, deliverance, and security have already been prayed for you. Our continued prayer for you is Ephesians 1:17-19: *That the God of our Lord Jesus Christ, the Father of glory, may give to you the spirit of wisdom and revelation in the knowledge of Him, the eyes of your understanding being enlightened; that you may know what is the hope of His calling, what are the riches of the glory of His inheritance in the saints, and what is the exceeding greatness of His power toward us who believe, according to the working of His mighty power.* May God bless you as you discover real balance, joy, and accountability in your life.

Throughout this journey, we will share our personal stories with you through the weekly devotions. Our experiences strongly influenced and encouraged us throughout the process of completing this curriculum. We hope and pray that you can relate and see yourself within the pages of this workbook and in the class discussions.

We would like to challenge you to fully commit to this journey. We will be asking you to take an in depth look at your life and make a real heartfelt commitment to create positive change. The **D*I*V*A*S Make-Up** is the mission of this curriculum. It lists all the benefits you will receive from this Life-Coaching curriculum if you do your part.

For the next eight weeks, set aside 30 to 40 minutes each day to complete the devotions. Each devotion ends with a DIV section. This section outlines the first steps in the DIVAS process.

- **DEVOTED** — Reading God's Word every day.

- **INDIVIDUALS** — Gaining personal insights and instructions from God's Word and answering questions designed to help you apply God's principles in your life.

- **VIA** — Prayer! This is the key to your success. If you will invest time in prayer over the next eight weeks, you will have a more intimate relationship with the Master. You will be fully equipped for every good work He has prepared for you.

At the end of each week you will be assigned an accountability partner from class. If you are completing this study as an individual, we encourage you to find a person to hold you accountable by asking the questions provided. This person will also be helpful in discussing the insights and instructions you are gaining as a result of the devotions.

- **ACCOUNTABILITY** — Weekly questions are provided to keep you on track and to allow you to develop transparent relationships with other sisters in Christ.

- **SPIRITUAL GROWTH** — You will be taking small steps to make positive changes over the next eight weeks. This section will provide a strong foundation for continued growth in your Christian walk.

A D∗I∗V∗A∗S Covenant is included in your material. This covenant is an agreement with you and your class participants. We encourage you to uphold these traits throughout this program. We also suggest you use this covenant as an agreement between you and your future accountability partner or group.

We recommend purchasing the D∗I∗V∗A∗S Walk of Purpose Journal by the end of Week Six. This tool will ensure continued success in achieving balance, joy, and accountability in your life. It maintains the D∗I∗V∗A∗S tools used in this curriculum and follows the same D∗I∗V∗A∗S process you will learn in the study.

We share some other options to help support you in your continued spiritual growth. These events can be church-wide or maintained with just a couple of D∗I∗V∗A∗S.

JEWEL NIGHT

A **Jewel Night** is simply a designated time and place for you or your group to hold accountability meetings. The structure is designed for a one-hour meeting consisting of a fifteen minute group devotion followed by individual and small group accountability. This is also a great way to build your D∗I∗V∗A∗S network within your church. **Jewel Night** provides opportunities for different classes to fellowship, bond, and meet other potential accountability partners. (Additional information is available in the Leader's Guide.)

SPA DAY

SPA stands for Spiritually Pampering Activity. This quarterly event is designed to bring women together to celebrate their accomplishments from the previous quarter. There are many options on how to facilitate these meetings. We offer several examples in the Leader's Guide. **SPA DAYS** are imperative to the success of the women participants truly living out God's individual missions in their lives. These events have a four-part focus.

- A time to provide encouragement among D∗I∗V∗A∗S through testimonies of progress and struggles.

- An opportunity to further equip the ladies in their spiritual growth.

- A time for personal reflection to examine current and future goals.

- An opportunity to write new goals and accountability questions for the next quarter.

We hope you will find the tools in this curriculum to be the beginning steps to living a life of balance, joy, and accountability – this is the life God has designed for you!

Let's get started....

D∗I∗V∗A∗S Defined

Devoted

D∗I∗V∗A∗S of the Divine are committed to placing the issues, concerns, and desires of their accountability group or partner above their own. They understand and live out sisterly love with honor and respect.

Individuals

D∗I∗V∗A∗S of the Divine are willing to take full responsibility for their life choices, regardless of their past or current circumstances. They surrender everything for the glory of God, allowing Him to heal and use their weakness and brokenness for the ministry He has set before them.

Via

D∗I∗V∗A∗S of the Divine desire to deepen their relationships with God through daily prayer and transparent relationships with other sisters in Christ.

Accountability

D∗I∗V∗A∗S of the Divine are willing to be accountable to God's Word and to encourage fellow sisters in Christ to do the same. They search out the truth in God's Word, apply it to every facet of their lives, and share God's truth in love with fellow D∗I∗V∗A∗S.

Spiritual Growth

D∗I∗V∗A∗S of the Divine are willing to make the necessary changes and commitments in their patterns of thoughts and actions to live up to the standards God has set before them. They know Spiritual Growth only occurs with change!

True D∗I∗V∗A∗S of the Divine are dedicated individuals who are willing to be transparent, honest, humble, and accountable to another sister in Christ in order to grow spiritually into all that God has called them to be!!

Are you ready to become one of the

D∗I∗V∗A∗S of the DIVINE?

D·I·V·A·S Make-Up

You will gain scriptural knowledge on joy, balance, personal accountability.

*

You will reach a clearer understanding of Christian commitment in all aspects of your life.

*

 You will uncover the power and passion of a purposeful prayer life.

*

You will discover the importance of living a life of godly purpose, one step at a time.

*

You will establish a greater sense of self through an in-depth assessment.

*

You will examine your past and discover your unique identity in Christ.

*

You will determine your life commitments and priorities through devotional exercises.

*

You will gain the ability and courage to simplify life choices by establishing goals.

*

You will expand your desire and dedication to surrender all aspects of your life to God's will.

*

You will develop a true God-driven mission for your life and establish practical ways to accomplish your purpose through accountable relationships.

*

You will build a real fellowship among Christian women through group activities and individual disclosure.

*

You will gain the tools and knowledge necessary for continued spiritual growth.

D∗I∗V∗A∗S Covenant

I _____, on this day of _____

_____, choose to become one of the D∗I∗V∗A∗S of the Divine. In doing so, I enter into a covenant to join other D∗I∗V∗A∗S, and soar to new heights in our relationship with God as we grow together through the process of accountability.

As one of the D∗I∗V∗A∗S I agree to be:

RELIABLE

I will attend the weekly sessions and treat each group meeting as a priority in my schedule, including being prompt to all sessions. I will contact the group leader if an absence is unavoidable, because God instructs us to be accountable. (*So then, each of us will give an account of himself to God.* Romans 14:12 NIV)

CONFIDENTIAL

I will provide a safe place among other D∗I∗V∗A∗S as we all seek a life of purity, integrity, character development, emotional stability, and assistance to others in handling temptations. Group conversations will remain in complete confidence in order to build trust and honor among us. (*Keep your heart with all diligence, for out of it springs the issues of life.* Proverb 4:23 NKJV)

MOTIVATOR

I will be an encourager to my D*I*V*A*S girlfriends through our accountability phone calls and homework assignments as each of us needs Godly girlfriends with whom we can freely share the deep issues of our hearts. (*I long to see you so that I may impart to you some spiritual gift to make you strong – that is, that you and I may be mutually encouraged by each others faith.* Romans 1:11-12 NIV)

TEACHABLE

I will seek and share biblical truth to questions and/or opinions during group discussions and accountability phone calls. (*All scripture is God-breathed and is useful for teaching, rebuking, correcting, and training in righteousness, so that the man of God may be thoroughly equipped for every good work.* 2 Timothy 3:16-17 NIV)

INTEGRITY

I commit to complete honesty through accountability discussions with other Godly D*I*V*A*S. (*If we confess our sins, he is faithful and just and will forgive us our sins and purify us from all unrighteousness.* 1 John 1:9 NIV)

ACCOUNTABLE

Let God be my ultimate accountability partner through a personal relationship with him that is deepened by prayer, reading the Word, and daily quiet time with Him. (*Take your everyday, ordinary life — your sleeping, eating, going to work, and walking around life — and place it before God as an offering.* Romans 12:1 MSG)

WEEK 1

D*I*V*A*S DIRECTIONS
BIBLICAL GUIDELINES FOR ACCOUNTABILITY

DAY 1 • Account-a-what-a?
Donna

"Accountability partner? What is that and what do I have to do?" That was my response the first time I was approached about this subject.

"Well, basically," she began, "I am working on some changes in my life. I have a new Life Purpose Statement, along with five roles or areas of my life that are important to me. I've taken each role and established 90-day goals that will help me become who and what I want to be in three years. For me to accomplish these goals, I've been asked to come up with someone who can help keep me on task and focused. Blah . . . Blah . . .Blah. Basically I need you, if you are willing, to call one time a week for about ten minutes and ask me these three questions."

"That's it — one ten minute phone call and three questions? Of course I can do that. Why didn't you just say that in the beginning?" I felt like I had better do this; she'd shared with me that she had been praying for over two weeks, and I was the only name that continued to come to her. This was intriguing to me because I honestly did not know anything about this person except her name. In fact, this was the first one-on-one conversation we had ever had. We had met about six months earlier. We attended the same church and small group class. We had never discussed anything other than her asking me to be a part of the new women's ministry team.

This was the basis of our relationship. The day she asked me to be her accountability partner we both wondered why God had brought us together in such a unique way. We aren't wondering today!

Little did we know or understand the depth of that 10-minute-1-time-a-week-3-question phone call. It was a divine weekly appointment that brought us full circle into becoming Devoted Individuals through Accountability and Spiritual growth (D*I*V*A*S).

As we began our 10-minute-1-time-a-week-3-question phone call, she shared with me in more detail how she had created and established her list of goals. I was intrigued and asked her to share her resources.[1] I wanted to clarify and understand how this goal setting process worked. I must admit I wasn't completely convinced I wanted to get that specific and that detailed about my life. However, from my background and other experiences, I knew some form of purpose and goals in life are necessary. Otherwise, life just happens. You wake up one day and look back and say, "Why didn't I do this when I was younger," or "I wish I had spent more time on this or that." So, I began jotting down some goals that I wanted to accomplish. They were simple goals. Most of us have similar goals but never really write them down or focus on them. For me, it was more or less the ordinary things you expect to accomplish in life, like pay off your house early, get out of debt, eat healthy, raise good kids, and have a good marriage.

I was going through this process, putting very little effort into it, when some very unexpected events unfolded in my life. (On another day I will share more details of these events with you.) These events were life-changing and eye-opening for me. They caused me to take a closer look at my life and re-examine it from an eternal perspective. They made me realize just how important living a life with purpose is. Several scriptures spoke louder than ever to me in different areas of my life. Scriptures like: Philippians 1:6: *Being confident of this very thing, that He who has begun a good work in you will complete it until the day of Jesus Christ* and Psalm 37:5: *Commit your way to the Lord; trust also in Him: and He shall bring it to pass.*

The story of Mary and Martha revealed to me many clues in my day-to-day life that I needed to change. I was busy trying to get it all done my way, trying to please God with my works (Martha). I was so wrapped up in the "work" part of my life that I forgot the worship part of my spiritual walk. I had to become more like Mary and enjoy Jesus in my day-to-day life. I had to stop working so hard at doing it my way. I had to start spending time with Jesus every day through prayer and Bible study to figure out His way in my life.

It's funny how God will get your attention. I knew that He was working in my life, because the same questions continued to pop-up all around me from different sources. We often hear these questions, answer half-heartedly and go on without much more thought. They're questions like: What do you want to be known for? What kind of a legacy do you want to leave? What do you want people to say about you at your funeral?

For me, the legacy I want to leave for my children and my grandchildren is very clear. The words that I want spoken about me at my own funeral are the words I heard spoken about someone. Yet at that point in my life, I knew that if I died that day neither my legacy nor the words spoken of me would be what I wanted. So, I went back to those ordinary goals I had jotted down on paper and re-wrote them with an eternal perspective. I was very passionate about making these changes in my life. They were by no means huge or difficult changes, but they were a start. It was the first step I took to living my life with a true sense of purpose and direction.

I shared these small steps with my phone-call partner. She helped me come up with my own three questions. Now we have a 20-minute-1-time-a-week-6-question phone call; a phone call that we choose not to live without!

Yes, *accountability* is a big word that can be very scary to many of us. However, it's a simple concept. It's a biblical concept. It's a life-changing concept. It is necessary in your life if you are going to live a life with Godly purpose, the life that you were created to live.

1 Peter 1:22

Since you have purified your souls in obeying the truth through the Spirit in sincere love of the brethren, love one another fervently with a pure heart.

1 Peter 5:5-6

Likewise you younger people, submit yourselves to your elders. Yes, all of you be submissive to one another, and be clothed with humility, for God resists the proud, but gives grace to the humble.

Romans 12:10-13

Be kindly affectionate to one another with brotherly love, in honor giving preference to one another; not lagging in diligence, fervent in spirit, serving the Lord; rejoicing in hope, patient in tribulation, continuing steadfastly in prayer; distributing to the needs of the saints, given to hospitality.

Devoted

Read 1 Peter 1:2, 5:5; Romans 12:10-13.

Individual

What insights, instructions, or inspirations do you feel God is saying to you?

_____

_____

_____

_____

_____

_____

_____

_____

Via – Prayer

Write a prayer asking God to guide you in your journey through this class.

_____

_____

_____

_____

_____

_____

_____

DAY 2 • Powerful Account-a-what-a

Sherri

Accountability is powerful. It makes me strive and continue to reach for goals that otherwise, would be too easy to let go. When my days are fast-paced and go, go, go from the start, I could easily decide that today is not the day that I will exercise, or today I will sleep late and not get up in time to have my devotions and prayer time before work. But when I know that I am going to "report" to someone about what I said I would do for the week, it motivates me to push on when I really don't want to.

For years, I have worked on goals and had my own personal mission statement. This has been a part of my life since college due to the different companies that I have worked for that encourage their employees to focus on goals in order to be more balanced with their work and personal lives. However, I never had real "accountability" for my goals. I was only accountable to myself! Yes, of course there are goals that must be achieved in our work lives, but I had never thought about having someone I could "report to" concerning my spiritual goals or my financial goals, or even my health and fitness goals. We talk about these things with our spouses, families or girlfriends, but we don't typically talk about a list of specific goals with a list of specific people. I think when we are talking about these "issues" with family or friends, we don't think anything about the word accountability. We're just basically having a conversation about "life."

If you agree to commit to becoming accountable to someone, you will be amazed and blessed at what will happen in your life. When I began to re-design how my goals were written on paper, I decided I needed/wanted to be more specific with my spiritual goals. I did not even know who to seek out as an accountability partner. For months, I prayed that God would put someone in my path who would become that person for me. I asked Him to open my eyes and give me awareness in my surroundings, in the conversations I had with people so I could begin to recognize who that person would be for me. I began to really focus on the people in my small group class. This is when I began to observe my future accountability partner! She had such a sweet spirit. I could tell she spent time focusing on God: She did devotions with her children and she was committed to the small group class homework or study guides that our class was asked to do. But I didn't personally know her. So, I began to ask God if she was the person He wanted me to talk with about accountability. As I continued to pray about my spiritual accountability partner, her name continued to pop up in my prayers. And let me just say that I was not immediately obedient! I was scared. Was I willing to talk with her and let her know I had some spiritual insecurities? If she agreed to talk with me weekly and help me work toward my spiritual goals, she would see my weaknesses. Would she think less of me? Was I willing to be vulnerable to that? Would she even want to schedule time to talk with me weekly? Did she even know what accountability was? Was she a goal-driven person, and could she relate to me?

One Sunday I finally approached her to ask if we could meet and if I could talk with her about my spiritual goals. It's been bliss ever since! Well, I laughingly have to confess — that is not exactly true. She has challenged me at times I didn't want to be challenged. She has pointed out some hard-core observations I needed to look at within myself. However, everything we have worked on or talked about has been in a true spirit of Christ-centered friendship. She has become invaluable in my life, and I now look forward to our conversations every Monday morning at 6:30 A.M.

We do have differences. We come from different backgrounds. I was the cheerleader in school, and she was the basketball player. I was more comfortable in dress-up clothes and fingernail polish. She was more comfortable in jeans, standing her ground on the ball field against the boys. But my fabulous accountability partner and I also have many similarities in our desire to be strong Christian women and to focus on the things in our lives that we know are pleasing to God. This has been the bond that has developed our friendship.

She is so much more to me now than just an accountability partner. She is a trusted friend who I know will be honest with me, who will guide me down the right path, and who is okay with letting me know in a kind way if I veer off course.

Work with us! Open your mind and heart to the possibility of having a real transparent, honest, and accountable friend in your life. Keep this at the forefront of your mind as we meet over the next several of weeks.

Devoted

Read Romans 15:14, Galatians 5:13-15, Colossians 3:16.

Individual

What insights, instructions, or inspirations do you feel God is saying to you? Today, take some time to write down any questions you may have about what accountability is, what it means, how it works, or any concerns you have, etc.

_____

_____

_____

_____

Via - Prayer

Ask God today to put someone in your path who will become your accountability partner. Ask Him to open your eyes and give you awareness in your surroundings and in the conversations you have with people, so you can begin to recognize who that person will be in your life.

Romans 15:14

Now I myself am confident concerning you, my brethren, that you also are full of goodness, filled with all knowledge, able also to admonish one another.

Galatians 5:13-15

For you, brethren have been called to liberty; only do not use liberty as an opportunity for the flesh, but through love serve one another. For all the law is fulfilled in one word, even in this: "You shall love your neighbor as yourself." But if you bite and devour one another, beware lest you be consumed by one another.

Colossians 3:16

Let the word of Christ dwell in you richly in all wisdom, teaching and admonishing one another in psalms and hymns and spiritual songs, singing with grace in your hearts to the Lord. And whatever you do in word or deed, do all in the name of the Lord Jesus, giving thanks to God the Father through Him.

Jewels of Accountability

Accountability can take on many different formats. In D*I*V*A*S we establish four different types of Accountability Groups. It is important to pray for God to show you which jewel will best fit your current circumstances.

DIAMOND

Diamonds are specifically renowned as a material with superlative, brilliant qualities. Diamond Accountability is a one-on-one relationship with another sister in Christ. When each woman is willing to openly and honestly share with the other, this accountability relationship can be equally as brilliant and radiant as the most perfectly cut diamond. This is a relationship in which each woman is striving to achieve certain goals in her life that she has determined at the end of our eight-week study. This one-on-one, weekly accountability is designed to allow women to offer each other positive encouragement in celebrating each other's accomplishments as well as to provide support and suggestions for overcoming obstacles and struggles. This can be accomplished with a scheduled 30-minute phone call.

RUBY

Rubies represent warmth and passion for mankind. Ruby Accountability is an accountability relationship among 3 or 4 women. So, this accountability group is the perfect way to express your victories and struggles with your goals and to receive unbridled love and encouragement from each other. In order to have appropriate time allotted for each person, this small group should be no more than four D*I*V*A*S. Each person in the group may be working on different goals. Each person will be given the same amount of time to share and get feedback from the group. This can be accomplished with a face-to-face meeting scheduled weekly, or no less than twice each month.

SAPPHIRE

Sapphires are used in many jeweled settings because of their remarkable hardness. Some sapphires are heat-treated to enhance their appearance, color, and clarity. Sapphire Accountability is designed to be a mentoring relationship. You may have a certain situation in your life that you are struggling with and you may want to seek out a "mentor" to advise you and "enhance" your current situation with clarity and positive guidance. This would be a woman who has already been through the same situation that you are currently experiencing. With her knowledge and experience she can guide you through your struggle with a biblical outlook. Together you determine the frequency of your conversations and create your own structure for the relationship.

AMETHYST

Amethyst is credited with many attributes throughout history. It has been called the stone of the mind as it brings calmness and clarity and quickens intelligence. Amethyst Accountability is set up as a mastermind group, a group of six to eight women who will brainstorm with each other about a certain topic, goal, or issue. Each woman may bring a different topic to the session, or the group may be put together based on the same goal that each woman is working toward (i.e. improving their marriages). An Amethyst Accountability group helps brainstorm ideas to help you move forward. It will provide you with enthusiasm and additional accountability. Thirty minutes should be devoted to each person's specific topic, so keep that in mind when deciding the number of women in this group. The group may determine the frequency of the meetings and the format, however each meeting should give the opportunity to share victories of accomplishment from the previous meeting, and each person in the group should continually build each other up with words of encouragement to confirm each other's success and confidence.

DAY 3 • Cover Girl

Sherri

Each morning I begin by applying my make-up mask,
"Why the new transformation?" the question YOU always ask.
I begin the cover-up process starting with a powdered base
To hide all of the blemishes not accepted by the "perfect" race.

After the make-up is complete, I accessorize myself for the day
With handbag, jewelry, and shoes to coordinate in the most fashionable way.
I only wear my clothes in the trendiest colors and hues
A D*I*V*A is what I want to be, but my focus is fashion and hair do's.

They want to see a girlfriend who is pretty, perfect and pure
But if they looked deep within, they'd see the me that's insecure.
I pretend that I am always joyous, happy and okay
Because I am concerned about what others have to say.

But the inner me is what I need an authentic girlfriend to see
And love me for the way I am because that's how You designed me.
Forgiving, supportive, and constantly there is the kind of love You give
This is the motto that I want my girlfriends and me to live!

Help me find that friend who can see me through Your eyes
And love me unconditionally and see through my disguise.
A fashion statement complete with make-up, clothes and hair
Let her see past faux perfection to the me that's really there.

Underneath the layers of make-up, the real me she will see
But please be patient with me as I reveal my mystery.
Together as true D*I*V*A*S, let us release all vanity and pride
And live our life with eternal perspective taking it all in stride.

Donna

This is a beautiful poem. In this society being who you really are isn't easy, much less realistic. We have each experienced hurt and loss. We each have our own insecurities, imperfections, and fears. And even though the majority of these insecurities, imperfections, and fears are very common among all of us, we rarely, if ever, share them with each other.

Instead, we have become great make-up artists — very good at disguising who we are and what we really feel. Yes, we are very clever. In fact, we are rather ingenious in the many ways we are able to paint, remold, and redecorate who we are. We have all worn our own make-up disguises. They may each be different, but they serve the same purpose. No matter their shade, we still use them to hide, to fit in, to feel normal, to be different, or to cover up the real person.

• What are some "disguises" women use to cover up who they really are? _____

_____

• Which "faux perfection" do you use most often?

_____

_____

_____

• Why do you think it is so hard to be who you really are?

_____

_____

_____

• List your biggest fear about revealing your "mystery."

_____

_____

_____

_____

Taking off the many layers is a brave thing to do. It might cause some uncomfortable feelings of vulnerability, guilt, shame, hurt, or even brokenness. You are not alone in these feelings.

Today we want to leave you with God's comforting words, His promises to you from Scripture. Use these verses as your sword to stand against those feelings as you continue on this journey in your life.

Devoted

Read the following scriptures. Underline words that comfort or inspire you.

1 Peter 5:10 *May the God of all grace, who called us to His eternal glory by Christ Jesus, after you have suffered a while, perfect, establish, strengthen, and settle you.*

1 Peter 1:6 *In this you greatly rejoice, though now for a little while, if need be, you have been grieved by various trials.*

Isaiah 61:1-3 *The Spirit of the Lord GOD is upon Me, because the LORD has anointed Me to preach good things to the poor; He has sent Me to heal the brokenhearted, to proclaim liberty to the captives, and the opening of the prison to those who are bound. . . .To comfort all who mourn, to console those who morn in Zion, to give them beauty for ashes, the oil of joy for mourning, the garment of praise for the spirit of heaviness; That they may be called trees of righteousness, the planting of the Lord that He may be glorified.*

2 Corinthians 4:16-18 *We do not lose heart. Even though our outward man is perishing, yet the inward man is being renewed day by day. For our light affliction, which is but for a moment, is working for us far more exceeding and eternal weight of glory, while we do not look at the things which are seen, but at things which are not seen. For the things which are seen are temporary, but the things which are not seen are eternal.*

Individual

What insights, instructions, or inspirations do you feel God is saying to you?

_____

_____

_____

_____

_____

Via – Prayer

Write a prayer asking God to "release all vanity and pride" and to help you live with an eternal perspective.

_____

_____

_____

_____

_____

* * *

DAY 4 • "Fear Not" a Piece of Paper
Donna

In group time this past week you participated in the Paper Days activity. You ended up with a bunch of torn paper in your hands. This paper was not yours. It didn't belong to you. You did not ask for it.

At the same time, you tore off pieces of your own paper and handed them to different group members. You might know some of the group members very well; you might not even know others' last names.

Perhaps that piece of paper represents what you are feeling at this point in your life: You are spread too thin. You can't keep it together yourself, much less give more of yourself toward putting someone else "back together." You might even be feeling the need to step out of this program before you get in over your head. Rest assured you are not alone. Consider the follwing:

> We must not wait until we are healed first, loved first, and then reach out. We must serve no matter how little we have our act together. It may well be that one of the first steps toward our own healing will come when we reach out to someone else.
>
> ~ Rebecca Manley Pippert, *Out of the Salt Shaker* [2]

Do you have some fears and hesitations about continuing in this program? Maybe you don't want to be transparent. You might not be willing to share your insecurities (take off the make-up). You might even be thinking, "I can't handle one more 'friend'."

Your reasons could be more personal: You don't feel "close enough to God" to commit to an accountability partner; you think your past is too "bad" even for God to use; your "pain" is too fresh to bear the thought of sharing it. The list can go on and on. You could probably write some fears I haven't even thought of. I am not going to try to convince you that your fears are not justifiable, because some of them might be. With our limited human understanding and the craftiness and schemes of the devil, we could all find a fear big enough, legit enough, for us to discontinue.

- Stop for a minute and list your fears as you confess them to God — He knows what you are feeling anyway.

_____

_____

_____

_____

_____

Now read and meditate on the verses in the sidebar.

God's Word says "fear not." Does that mean this journey could be a little scary or a little uncomfortable? Absolutely! I am sure Abram felt these same fears when God told him to pack up and leave all that he had ever known and to venture into the unknown. The shepherds in the field were told to "fear not" when a host of angels (not just one) appeared to them to share the good news of Jesus' birth. I am sure, in fact, I'm positive they felt a little uncomfortable and a little scared.

"Fear not." God is speaking those very words to you right now.

Rick Warren explains "fear not" in this way:

> No one wants what's best for you more than God. No one knows better what will make you truly happy! God doesn't want you to be afraid of Him. He wants you to run *to* Him, not *from* Him. In fact, 365 times in the Bible, God says, "Don't be afraid!" That's one "Fear not" for every day of the year! So what are you afraid of?[3]

In other words, God is saying, "You may experience fear but depend on Me and I will show you what will make you truly happy — despite the fear."

If you "fear not" and are obedient, then you will enjoy all that God has prepared for you. You will become all that God has created you to be.

We know these things are God's will in your life because this is what God's Word says. In other words, those pieces of paper are God's will in your life. They are your responsibility. God will show you how to "put back" those pieces of paper. He will also allow someone in your life to "put back" your pieces to help you become whole in Jesus Christ. If this is God's plan for your life, you can have faith that He has prepared a way for it to become a part of your life. "Fear not" and commit yourself to this journey and commit yourself to God's call in your life.

Isaiah 35:4
Say to those who are fearful-hearted, "Be strong, do not fear!"

Psalms 118:6
The LORD is on my side; I will not fear. What can man do to me?

2 Kings 6:16
So he answered, "Do not fear, for those who are with us are more than those who are with them."

Judges 6:23
Then the Lord said to him, "Peace be with you; do not fear, you shall not die."

Deuteronomy 31:6
Be strong and of good courage, do not fear nor be afraid of them; for the LORD your God, He is the One who goes with you. He will not leave you, nor forsake you.

Deuteronomy 3:22
You must not fear them, for the LORD your God Himself fights for you.

Devoted

Read the scriptures on fear again.

Individual

What insights, instructions, or inspirations do you feel God is saying to you?

_____

_____

_____

_____

_____

Via – Prayer

Write a prayer asking God to help you "fear not" this journey you are on.

_____

_____

_____

_____

_____

_____

* * *

DAY 5 • Eternal Perspective

Donna

I shared with you earlier in another devotion how I had experienced several life-changing events that made me take a closer look at my life and what I was living for. These events encouraged me to become more purposeful, more devoted, and more Christ-like in my day-to-day life. I don't know what is going on in your life at this time. You could be participating in this study for several reasons. You might be at a season of change in your life, and ready to move forward. You might be here because you have always wanted to set goals and have a Life Purpose Statement, because that is what successful people do. You might even be here simply because it sounded like a lot of fun. Regardless of your reason, you can know this for sure — you are right where God wants you to be, and our hope and prayer is for you to start living your life with eternal perspective.

Eternal perspective: It's a neat sounding phrase. The idea sounds important. It even sounds a tad biblical. What does it mean to you? Are you living with an eternal perspective? Are you living your life daily thinking about the effects your day will have on eternity? Are you living your life daily striving for eternal riches? Are you living your life daily trying to extend your eternal family? I must say that I wasn't doing a good job of this until God sent me an eternal perspective check-up.

One year my life was very challenging and full of loss. Within four months of each other my husband's grandmother and grandfather went to be with the Lord. G-paw, as my kids called him, died unexpectedly of a massive heart attack on December 17th. G-maw, his wife, died on May 30th after a three-year battle with cancer. These two people were very dear to me. I married into the family, but they were my grandparents as well. We lived next to them for the first three years of our marriage. I had a very special bond with both of them. G-maw and I could lay in the sun all day long at the beach and never run out of things to talk about. (And we did just that more times than I can even try to count.) G-paw, well, there are not words to describe that man!! I think they said it best at his funeral — he loved golf, he loved his family and he loved God. He was a simple man, but if you knew him you knew this was true about him. Since G-paw's death was so unexpected, we all (the family) stopped, as most of us do in a time like this, and remembered how precious each day is and how we are not promised another one. For the next few weeks we lived with this new perspective. We made sure we called each other and told each other how much we loved one another. We never left each other's sight without a long embrace. It was a hard time, but we leaned on one another.

We continued to live with this new perspective for the next several months because each of us knew G-maw's battle was coming to an end. We gathered around her and supported her through several close calls in the hospital. We were not even sure she was going to make it to the New Year. We had to put her in the hospital on Christmas Day. G-maw battled through until Easter. She stopped her chemo and fought courageously to get her strength back enough to be able to walk. G-maw had a passion and a deep love for salt air and sandy beaches. The family told her we would take her to the beach one more time if she could walk. With lots of love, support, and most importantly, prayer, she gained enough strength to walk again. The family: her three children and their spouses, her five grandkids, her two grand-daughter-in-laws (that is what she called us) and her four great-grandchildren were able to go for a week to her favorite place – Garden City, South Carolina.

That was the most memorable vacation I have ever had. It was special in many ways. We each appreciated and thanked God everyday for the family that was there. We each soaked in every moment we could with G-maw because we knew it would be our last trip with her. We stayed up late and got up early just to squeeze every moment we could out of that week. We stopped as a family (all 18 of us), to pray, and offer up thanksgiving and praise because we knew we were experiencing a miracle on this trip: She was not even supposed to be out of the hospital; her body had already begun the dying process. We came home, and within a week she went to the glorious beaches of Heaven.

G-maw loved her family – especially the great-grandchildren. She called me every Monday morning to make sure I was bringing my daughter or son by to stay with her while I went to exercise. It never failed when I went to pick the kids up she insisted we go out for lunch. Of course, we often had to stop by the store to pick up this or that while we were out. It was almost always a given: Mondays were spent with G-maw. I must admit, there were many Mondays that I had something else I needed to do other than run around town. There was always the laundry, house cleaning, mowing the grass. The "life" things that always need your attention.

My kids loved her. She got down on the floor and sat through numerous imaginary dinners. She played shopping and dress up. One of my daughter's favorite games was to play dress-up with the gray wig G-maw wore when she lost her hair. They each took turns putting it on and seeing which one could make the silliest face. It was a side-splitting competition to say the least. Even my son got in on the action. In fact, the game was so much fun that the whole family played as we gathered around her bedside during those final few days. Yes, we all played, from the oldest child down to the six month old. (I have pictures to prove it!) G-maw was a beautiful soul!

As her final moments were approaching, we gathered around her bedside and started to pray. During this prayer her breathing started changing and we all knew it was almost over. My children (five and three years old at the time) had just awakened from their naps. My son came walking in to the living room. He looked up at me with his innocent eyes and said, "I want to see G-maw." I wanted to protect him but I also wanted him to be able to say goodbye. He was adamant about seeing her. I explained to him that G-maw could not open her eyes and look at him but she could hear anything he said. We could hear her labored breathing in the living room where we were standing, and I explained to him that she was okay. He still wanted to go in to see her. I carried him in and he held her hand and said, "I love you G-maw." With every last bit of energy she could muster, she squeezed his little hand and tilted her head toward his voice. My daughter soon followed into the room. She climbed up at the foot of her bed and began to rub G-maw's feet. She would just grin and say, "I love you G-maw." My daughter stayed there and held G-maw's foot until we took her out of the room. Within seconds of her leaving, G-maw took her last breath.

I thank God for all those Mondays. I can't tell you the many "life" things I didn't accomplish on Mondays, but I can tell you the look on my child's face as he went into that room to see his beloved G-maw. He loved her so much he wanted to say goodbye, even during those final labored moments of her life. He loved her because she was such a big part of his life even at the tender age of three. He will still to this day tell me how much he misses her. My daughter has even asked if Jesus will come live in her heart so that when she dies she can go see G-maw and G-paw. Praise God for those Mondays!

G-maw loved the beach, she loved the sand, and she loved laying out in the sun; but I believe she loved these things for reasons we never really understood until those last weeks of her life. You see, she loved her beach trips because she surrounded herself with her family when she went. She loved those beach trips so much because she loved her time with the family. In those moments she did not have to compete with our jobs, our schedules, our ballgames, our church functions. She could have spent her money on bigger and better things for herself, but that was not what she treasured — it was her family.

Her love and dedication to her family was beautifully described at her Celebration of Life ceremony. Her son had prayed these words just hours before she passed: "Father, open the doors to your heavenly home so You can say to this dear child of Yours, 'Well done my child, welcome home.'" She was described as a Proverbs 31 woman. Her legacy will never be forgotten. She had not only invested so much love in my children that they wanted to be at her bedside in those final hours, she had also invested in the lives of everyone she encountered. During the days that followed we heard from many people about how they were touched by Mrs. Ruth...her love, her fight, and her never-wavering faith in her Savior. She lived with eternal perspective. She lived her life in such a way that her greatest accomplishments were expanding her eternal family, and her greatest riches are the crowns she will lay at the feet of Jesus.

- Does your daily life reflect an unwavering faith?

- Does your daily life reflect your desire for eternal treasures, or earthly riches?

- Will your family refer to you as a Proverbs 31 woman? (If you are not familiar with this passage, stop for a moment and read it.)

- What do you want said about you at your funeral?

- What legacy do you want to leave?

- Take a moment and write down the things you want to be known for when you die.

_____

_____

_____

If you died today, would this be true of your life?

Devoted

Read the following scriptures and underline the benefits of accountability.

Ecclesiastes 4:9-12

Two are better than one, Because they have a good reward for their labor. For if they fall, one will lift up his companion. But woe to him who is alone when he falls, For he has no one to help him up. Again if two lie down together, they will keep warm; But how can one be warm alone? Though one may be overpowered by another, two can withstand him. And a threefold cord is not quickly broken.

Proverb 11:14

Where there is no counsel, the people fall; But in the multitude of counselors there is safety.

Benefits of Accountability
- Two can stand better than one
- Safety from temptation
- Grow in wisdom
- Spirit of unity
- Correction
- Encouragement
- Wise counsel

Proverbs 13:14-20 NLT

The advice of the wise is like a life-giving fountain; those who accept it avoid the snares of death. A person with good sense is respected; a treacherous person is headed for destruction. Wise people think before they act; fools don't — and even brag about their foolishness. An unreliable messenger stumbles into trouble, but a reliable messenger brings healing. If you ignore criticism, you will end in poverty and disgrace; if you accept criticism you will be honored. It is pleasant to see dreams come true, but fools refuse to turn from evil to attain them. Walk with the wise and become wise; associate with fools and get in trouble.

Romans 15:1-6 NIV

We who are strong ought to bear with the failings of the weak and not to please ourselves. Each of us should please his neighbor for his good, to build him up. For even Christ did not please himself but, as it is written: "The insults of those who insult you have fallen on me." For everything that was written in the past was written to teach us, so that through endurance and the encouragement of the Scriptures we might have hope. May the God who gives endurance and encouragement give you a spirit of unity among yourselves as you follow Christ Jesus, so that with one heart and mouth you may glorify the God and Father of our Lord Jesus Christ.

Individual

How can accountability help you accomplish the things you want to be known for? _____

_____

_____

Via – Prayer

Begin your prayer today asking God for the right accountability partner for you.

Accountability

ACCOUNTABILITY PARTNER'S INFORMATION:

NAME: _____

PHONE: _____

       (home)   (cell)   (work)

EMAIL: _____

CONTACT DATE AND TIME: _____

Friendship Question:

Where is your favorite vacation spot?

Accountability Questions:

Did you complete your D*I*V*A*S devotionals this week?

What do you want to be said about you at your funeral? (Day 5)

Spiritual Growth

I will continue my spiritual growth this week by completing the following action(s):

1. _____

2. _____

3. _____

List items your partner(s) will be focusing on for the next week. Note any prayer requests from meeting.

1. _____

2. _____

3. _____

PRAYER FOR ACCOUNTABILITY PARTNER:

Father, as I begin this journey I pray you will guide me in discovering the right person who will be honest, humble, and transparent with me. O God, enlighten my spirit to the person who will speak Your truth to me, encourage me and support me in becoming all you created me to be. (Psalm 119:73-80 MSG)

WEEK 2

D*I*V*A*S DIALECT

DEVELOPING AN INTIMATE PRAYER LIFE

DAY 1 • Just Do It

Donna

I have been saved since I was a little girl. I have always prayed, and I have always believed in prayer. Like many of you, I have read and heard story after story of amazing answers to prayers, miraculous healings, testimonies of how God spoke to different people, and how God protected and guided people. However, until a few years ago that was all they were to me — stories. They weren't realities in my own life. I'm not saying I had never had my own prayers answered or personally felt God guiding or protecting me, because I have. I am talking about those really "good," really amazing stories — the give-you-chill-bumps kind.

How about you? Do you have really amazing personal stories of answered prayer? Are you moved daily by the way you see God answering prayer and working in your life? Or is your prayer life almost non-existent? Maybe prayer is just a list that you recite when you think about it.

If you had asked me those same questions several years ago I would have told you I didn't see God moving daily; it might be monthly or even quarterly at best. My prayer habit consisted of saying a blessing before meals and falling asleep as I recited my list to Him at night. (Sound familiar?)

Below, and continuing on the next page, describe your prayer life.

_____

_____

_____

_____

_____

One day, at a time we were planning a retreat at our church, I heard a sermon by my pastor on the power and importance of prayer in a believer's walk.

I had taken part in planning events at my previous church and with other organizations. They had all gone okay, but they had never had much impact.

I knew I was the same person planning this retreat as I had been when planning the other ones. I had the same abilities, the same education, the same know how. Now, though, I also realized there was only one way for this retreat to be any different or have more impact on God's kingdom than the others had. It had to come from the eternal!

How do you do that? Simple. Just like you would include any other member of the group, you invite God in on the planning. You ask Him for His wisdom, His guidance, His suggestions, His blessings. You delegate the hard stuff to Him; after all He can handle it. You delegate the small stuff to Him; after all it's important to Him. You delegate the confusing part to Him; after all He sees the big picture. Actually, you just go to Him daily with praises, thanksgiving, questions, guidance . . . .You seek His answer in the planning book that He wrote. You call down the promises He has already given you.

That is exactly what we did. We prayed Scripture. We prayed individually. We prayed as a group. We prayed for guidance. We prayed for strength. We prayed for energy. We prayed for the Holy Spirit to be with us. We prayed for the women who would be attending, even when we did not know who they were.

We prayed! Wow! Now I have those give-you-chill-bumps kind of stories!

If you ask me those same questions about my prayer life now, I will tell you, Yes, I see Him working daily in my life. I pray all the time, and about everything. I don't just recite my list to Him, I have a personal conversation between a father and a daughter.

So what changed? What Bible study did I do? How did I do it?

Here's my answer: "I just did it!" I just committed myself to pray every day, in every situation.

You can do it, too. You can have those chill-bump stories in your own life. So, just do it! Just pray! It is that simple.

Devoted

Read Ephesians 6:18, 1 Thessalonians 5:16-17, 1 Timothy 2:1.

Individual

What insights, instructions, or inspirations do you feel God is saying to you in these three verses?

_____

_____

_____

_____

_____

List three reasons why prayer is important to you.

_____

_____

_____

_____

List three ways you can improve your prayer life.

_____

_____

_____

_____

Ephesians 6:18

Praying always with all prayer and supplication in the Spirit, being watchful to this end with all perseverance and supplication for all the saints –

1 Thessalonians 5:16-18

Rejoice always, pray without ceasing, in everything give thanks; for this is the will of God in Christ Jesus for you.

1 Timothy 2:1

Therefore I exhort first of all that supplications, prayers, intercessions, and giving of thanks be made for all men.

Via - Prayer

Write a prayer of commitment to spend more time with God.

_____

_____

_____

_____

_____

* * *

DAY 2 • Be Yourself

Donna

First, just do it. Second, be yourself!

God knows who you are. Remember, He created you. He knew you before you knew yourself (Jeremiah 1:5). He knows every hair on your head, even the gray ones you struggle to cover up (Matthew 10:30). God knows what is in your heart, even the not-so-good stuff.

If God knows you this intimately, then why would you try to be something you are not when you go to Him in prayer?

As women we are in a society that forces us to compare ourselves to everyone else. Because we are so accustomed to comparing ourselves and judging ourselves, we try to conform to what everyone else is doing. Let's face it, ladies, we do this to the point that we are not sure who we truly are. We lack the confidence and the security to just be exactly who we are. This comparison factor is so ingrained in us that we carry this over into our prayer life as well.

Be honest with yourself. Have you ever heard another woman pray and thought to yourself, "I wish I could pray like that?" Of course you have. Have you ever spoken with someone who raves about her prayer journal and how she is so blessed because she has such a treasured history of all God has done for her? What about the lady who gets up at 5:30 every morning to pray for hours before her day even begins?

We all are guilty of comparing ourselves to these women. We want to have what they have, so we try to do it their way. But when all we get is frustration, discouragement, and dissatisfaction, we stop developing our prayer life all together.

My question to you is this: Why do we do this to ourselves? God is the one being who already knows us better than we know ourselves. Why do we try to go to Him as anything other than who we really are? Look at the people who prayed in the Bible. Did they do it all the same way? No. Can you imagine how long the book of Psalms would be If everyone who prayed wrote it down the way David did?

> In the Bible people prayed in various ways: sometimes with hands raised (see Psalm 28:2), sometimes kneeling (see Luke 22:41), or sometimes kneeling with their eyes lifted to heaven (1 Kings 8:54). At other times prayers were accompanied by singing (see Acts 16:25). There were prayers without words, silent prayers (see Joshua 6:16-20), and prayers that were sung to God, like those recorded in the Psalms. The pray-ers in the Bible didn't just pray at home. They changed locations, sometimes praying on mountaintops (see Exodus 19), inside and outside the temple (see Luke 1:8-10), in prison cells (see Acts 16:23-25), and even from inside a fish (see Jonah 2:1).
> Cheri Fuller, *A Busy Woman's Guide To Prayer*[4]

We're going to cover many different avenues of prayer in another devotion. For now I want you to describe what you believe is the best way for *you* to pray. What fits you, your personality, your schedule, your needs? Do you like ongoing chit-chat throughout your day? Do you prefer getting up early and getting it done? Do you prefer to unwind in prayer before bed time? Do you pray in the shower because it is the only place you're alone? Do you need to write it down in order to stay focused? Do you need to scream it out loud to relieve the tension or the pain? Do you need to cry out, or whisper silently? Do you need to be in a certain place before you can talk with God? Do you need to pray with others or be alone?

List the different ways you have prayed in the past.

_____

_____

_____

Which way(s) worked best for you?

_____

_____

In what way(s) might you change your prayer life to make it more effective? Consistent?

_____

_____

Is there a particular area you would like to explore in your prayer life? (journaling, praying at certain times, prayer closets . . .)

_____

_____

Devoted

Read Romans 8:26 and Matthew 18:19.

Individual

What do these verses say to you?

_____

_____

_____

_____

Romans 8:26
Likewise the Spirit also helps in our weaknesses. For we do not know what we should pray for as we ought, but the Spirit Himself makes intercession for us with groanings which cannot be uttered.

Matthew 18:19-20
Again I say to you that if two of you agree on earth concerning anything that they ask, it will be done for them by My Father in heaven. For where two or three are gathered together in My name, I am there in the midst of them.

Via – Prayer

Write a prayer asking God to help you just be yourself during your prayer time. Ask Him to give you a passion and desire to see and talk to Him as your friend.

_____

_____

_____

_____

* * *

DAY 3 • Enjoy the Relationship
Donna

Okay, by now you have decided to pray, and to pray in a way that "fits," or is the most comfortable to, you. The next important aspect of prayer is to remember to enjoy this beautiful relationship you are developing.

Yes, I know that sounds silly. How can you not enjoy spending time with God, talking with the Creator, the Master, the Almighty? Just the thought sounds good and it makes you feel good. So, why remind us to enjoy it?

Simple. Anything that requires that much of ourselves and our commitment is bound to cause some burnout, some stress, and some sense of an overwhelming burden. Think about all the things we need to pray about. We pray for God to guide us, protect us, bless us, transform us. What about our marriages, our children, our extended families, our pastors, our teachers, our country's leaders, our missionaries, our finances, our jobs, our schools, our troops, the sick, the lost, the hurting?

Now do you see what I mean? It seems to be overwhelming, and we haven't even started to list any of the personal "stuff" that is really close to your heart.

Do you feel burned out or overwhelmed when it comes to prayer?

_____

How do we avoid the "burden" of prayer?

To answer that question we must change our perspective on what prayer is. I think once you rediscover what it is in your life, then you will truly enjoy your prayer time and see it as much more than a burden or a duty. Seeing your prayer time as a way of building your relationship with the Almighty instead of a "to-do" list is the only way your prayer life will become personal.

Write your personal definition of prayer.

_____

_____

_____

Think about this: Do you know the President of the United States? Of course you do. You've seen him on TV; you've heard others talk about him (the good and the bad); you've probably read some articles about him. Some of you might have researched different aspects of his life or his character. You have a pretty good idea of who he is, right? Now, think about that special friend in your life…the best friend that you share everything and anything with. You know her so well you can predict what she's going to wear; what she's going to do; and yes, you can even finish her sentence. You can shop for her because you know not only her style, but her shoe size as well! You could venture to say you know both of these people. Obviously, you know your best friend better than the President.

Stop for a moment and write down all the many ways you have connected with this friend. Include shopping trips, inside jokes, and phone calls; but don't forget the struggles, the hardships, the true tests of friendship that you have gone through with her.

_____

_____

My question to you is this: Do you want to know God the way you know the President, or do you want to know God the way you know your best friend?

- Do you want to know Him by what others say, or do you want to know Him intimately, as you do your friend?
- Do you want to know Him so vastly you can sense what He will be saying to you next?
- Do you want to know Him so deeply you trust Him with your biggest weaknesses and greatest fears?
- Do you want to know Him so personally you can feel His presence with you wherever you go?
- Do you want to know Him so intimately His touch can bring you peace, healing, grace, mercy, understanding?

Do you want to know Him? There is only one way – PRAY!

Prayer is how we know God! Prayer is how we discover the essence of God. It is how we open ourselves to God's own self and presence. It is how we talk to God. It is how God talks to us. It is the means through which we discover one of the greatest treasures in our Christian walk. It is a treasure worth seeking out.

Don't become discouraged with prayer. Just commit yourself to do it, and find a way that "fits" you and your schedule. Once you begin your daily relationship with Jesus Christ, you will find a true enjoyment in the time you spend with Him, and you will long to get to know Him more and more. Prayer then becomes a true pleasure, not a "burden." So go ahead, get started enjoying the relationship.

PRAYER
is how we discover the essence of God!

Devoted

Read James 4:8, Jeremiah 33:3, 1 Peter 5:7, Ephesians 3:20.

Individual

After reading these scriptures, how does God work to deepen our friendship as we pray to Him?

_____

_____

_____

_____

_____

_____

_____

Via - Prayer

Write a letter to Jesus as if He was a friend you had not seen in a long time and wanted to reconnect with.

_____

_____

_____

_____

_____

_____

_____

_____

James 4:8

Draw near to God and He will draw near to you....

Jeremiah 33:3

'Call to me and I will answer you, and show you great and mighty things, which you do not know.'

1 Peter 5:7

Cast all your anxiety on him because he cares for you. (NIV)

Ephesians 3:20

Now to him who is able to do immeasurably more than all we ask or imagine, according to his power that is at work within us....(NIV)

Day 4 • Never-Ending Chit-Chat
Donna

"Okay God, it's 7:00 A.M. on Tuesday and I have this, this, and this, to do today. Could you give me this, this, and that to make it easier for me? Oh, and by the way, while I am out today, could you heal the sick and bless the poor? Thanks. I'll touch base with you in a few days. I'm pretty busy with the kids' ballgames, laundry, and the projects at work. I'll drop you an email if I need anything else."

I hope you're laughing, but this is probably not far from the truth of most of our prayer lives. It was a good representation of my prayer life until I made a few changes in the way I viewed prayer time.

Do you believe that once you invite Jesus in your heart, the Holy Spirit is with you always? (Ephesians 1:13)

Do you realize that the Holy Spirit goes to the mall, to the grocery store, to work with you? He is with you when you fold laundry; when you're cooking; when you're putting on your make-up in the morning; when you are driving; when you are waiting at the doctor's office; when you are shopping. Yes, He is with you.

Do you talk to Him when you're at these places or when you're doing these tasks? I didn't, until recently. I realized through some of my reading material and research, the concept of never-ending chit-chat. I shared this realization with a friend of mine, and we were both intrigued enough to try it.

We have very different day-to-day lives. She does not have children; however, she is very devoted to her career. In her free time she volunteers for several organizations. Her day is very structured and busy. I, on the other hand, don't know which way I am going, much less what is next on my to do list. My day changes from minute to minute. In just one hour I might go from cleaning peanut butter and jelly sandwiches off the wall to writing D•I•V•A•S curriculum for the church.

When we tried this new concept of infusing our day with prayer. We both were amazed at how awesome it was to be in constant communication with God all day. We both felt a deeper closeness, a deeper sense of God's presence throughout our days. We had more comfort, more peace, more encouragement, even on those crazy "nothing-goes-right" kind of days. We were more aware of God's glory all around us.

The best part of this never-ending chit-chat with God is that it is so simple. All you have to do is find prayer markers throughout your day and incorporate prayer each time one of these markers appears. The following are some great examples of simple prayer markers:

Folding Laundry:

> This is something most woman do in the course of a week. Use this time to pray for your family. Pray for the person who wears those socks or that shirt. By the time you have finished one load of laundry your whole family will have been prayed for.

Stopped at a Stop Sign or Light:

> Pray for a different leader each time you're waiting for the light to change. (President, government leaders, pastor, teachers, employer)

Taking a Shower:

> Pray for forgiveness and for God to remove any unclean area of your life. Think of it as a daily spiritual cleaning.

Passing a Police Station, School, Hospital or Church:

> Pray for our law enforcement, our teachers, our principals, the sick and hurting, our pastors.

Are you getting the idea? Take a few moments and write down four ways that you can infuse prayer into your day. Include the prayer markers that will remind you to pray and what you will be praying for. Be creative! Think about the many things in your life that are always on your prayer list. If you really want to add a punch to your prayer markers then find a scripture to pray at each marker. Don't be afraid to ask someone to help you find the right scripture to pray. There are many resources out there, and you can always look up the subject in a concordance. This is a great way to hide God's Word in your heart (Psalm 119:11) as well.

Prayer Subject: _____

    Prayer Marker: _____

        Scripture: _____

Prayer Subject: _____

    Prayer Marker: _____

        Scripture: _____

Prayer Subject: _____

    Prayer Marker: _____

        Scripture: _____

Prayer Subject: _____

    Prayer Marker: _____

        Scripture: _____

Devoted

Read the following verse and circle how often we are to pray.

1 Thessalonians 5:16-18

Rejoice always, pray without ceasing, in everything give thanks; for this is the will of God in Christ Jesus for you.

Individual

List some ways you can incorporate more conversations with God throughout your day.

_____

_____

_____

Via – Prayer

This verse doesn't seem so impossible when you involve yourself in never-ending chit-chat. Here is one more easy way to pray blessings for other people, from Cheri Fuller's book, *A Busy Woman's Guide to Prayer*[5]. It's quick, easy, and completely covers the person in all arenas of life. Practice by writing a BLESS prayer for your accountability partner and two other special people in your life.

B - Body (energy, strength, healing)

L - Labor (stress related to work, ministry projects, role responsibilities)

E - Emotion (courage, peace, endurance, discernment, wisdom)

S - Social (people around them, how they can impact, get along with, support them)

S - Spiritual Growth (God teach them, transform them, prepare them, guide them.)

B—Body   L—Labor   E-Emotion   S-Social   S-Spiritual Growth

Name of Person:
_____

- **B** _____
- **L** _____
- **E** _____
- **S** _____
- **S** _____

Name of Person:
_____

- **B** _____
- **L** _____
- **E** _____
- **S** _____
- **S** _____

Name of Person:
_____

- **B** _____
- **L** _____
- **E** _____
- **S** _____
- **S** _____

DAY 5 • Solitude
Donna

Among many Christian women today, there is a strange sort of logic that suggests that spiritual resource and renewal are found in constantly seeking new voices, attending more meetings, listening to incessant music, and gathering to exchange half-thought-out opinions. How often do we fall into the trap of believing that God is most pleased when we have maximized our information, our schedules, and our relationships? Disengagement means silence before God, first of all. It is a time of heavenly discussion during which we listen more than we speak. And silence demands solitude.

Gail MacDonald, *High Call, High Privilege*[6]

I completely understand how farfetched this sounds to some. However, here's the bottom line. If you don't listen, how do you know God's answer?

We need to listen more than we speak. Silence and solitude are great ideas, but we must be realistic. How many women do you know who listen more than they speak? How many women really have time for solitude?

In the last devotional we learned about never-ending chit-chat with God. This is a powerful principle, and very beneficial. However, I must share one very important warning with you about this never-ending chit-chat. I share this with you because when I first started using prayer markers and infusing prayer into my day, I found myself cutting back on my quiet time. I tried to convince myself that I had prayed all day and covered all the items on my prayer list, so there was no need to have my usual quiet time. I was so wrong! You see there is a very strong truth in the above quote. Heavenly discussion is a time where we listen more than we speak, and silence demands solitude. Remember this verse: Be still and know that I am God (Psalm 46:10)? God is saying be still and feel My presence, hear My voice, seek My will.

Sorry ladies, but we can't do that in five-minute prayers throughout the day. *We must find time to find God!* Quiet time, alone time — no cell phone, no kids — no interruption time. Just time for you and your heavenly Father. Do you find solitude in your day? If not, why?

_____

_____

How would 15 minutes of listening to God improve your walk?

_____

_____

Solitude is definitely not an easy task, nor will it come naturally to you. As wives, mothers, daughters, sisters, employees, friends, we have brain-overload...and it does not come with a pause button. It never stops. We go to bed thinking about things. We wake up thinking about things. Even when we try to have 15 minutes of solitude something always pops up...and off we go down the rabbit trail, chasing the "What's for supper?" rabbit. Then we stumble over the "Who's picking up the kids?" turtle. Finally, we fall off the rabbit trail into the "Oops, I forgot milk!" river. Ever been on that adventure?

Let's stop for a moment and see how well we can find solitude. Set a timer (most cell phones have one), and for the next five minutes try not to think about anything. Just focus on the essence of God. (Yes, I want you to do this!)

When the time's up, be honest with yourself, and write down all the things that popped up in your mind.

_____

_____

_____

Was that hard?
(Welcome back to those of you who fell asleep during your five minutes of solitude.)

It takes practice and patience, (and sometimes an act of Congress!). But silence and solitude are necessary in our prayer time and in our walk. If we want to know God, then we must experience Him, not just talk to Him.

Here are some guidelines for creating your personal quiet time with God (the time you listen, not talk.)

- End your prayer time or devotional time with 15 minutes of solitude. Your heart is prepared to experience God and listen to Him.

- Find a quiet, peaceful place. Some women actually walk or run during their solitude time. Be creative and do what works for you.

- Keep the time and place consistent to help you form a habit.

- Start with five minutes and work your way up to more time. This way you will not get discouraged.

When your mind drifts to your to-do list, refocus yourself by saying the following scripture prayer.

Psalm 46:10: *Be still and know that I am God.*

> Lord, I'm having a hard time being still. You know how much I have to do today, but I know I need to give You the tithe of time that belongs to You. I know the time I spend talking with You will help me to keep You first in my life. Let me re-focus my thoughts on You and Your loving kindness.

As we close this week on prayer, here is a quick summary for you:

Just pray! Pray your way! Pray all the time! Enjoy your prayer time! Really experience God in your prayers by listening!

We hope and pray that you have a new desire, dedication, and determination to make your time with God a unique and personal relationship.

Devoted

Read Proverbs 3:5-6 scripture and scripture prayer today.

Proverbs 3:5-6

Trust in the LORD with all your heart, And lean not on your own understanding; In all your ways acknowledge Him and He will direct your paths.

Scripture Prayer of Proverbs 3:5-6

Lord, I need to refocus my thoughts and put my trust in you and not worry about the things I need to complete on my to-do list. I know if I focus my quiet time on you, you will provide me with the answers I need to make it through my day.

Individual

What insights, individual instructions, or inspirations did you gain from this scripture today? How do you think this scripture prayer can help you calm your mind and listen as God speaks to you during your quiet time?

_____

_____

_____

_____

_____

_____

Via - Prayer

Make the scripture prayer from Proverbs 3:5-6 or Psalms 46:10 your prayer for today. As you spend some time just listening for God to speak to you, journal what you feel God is speaking to your heart.

_____

_____

_____

_____

_____

_____

_____

_____

Accountability

ACCOUNTABILITY PARTNER'S INFORMATION:

NAME: _____

PHONE: _____

      (home)   (cell)   (work)

EMAIL: _____

CONTACT DATE AND TIME: _____

Friendship Question:

How did your spouse propose to you? If you are not married, describe your dream proposal.

Accountability Questions:

Did you complete your D*I*V*A*S devotionals this week?

What is the biggest obstacle in your prayer life?

Spiritual Growth

I will continue my spiritual growth this week by completing the following action(s):	List items your partner(s) will be focusing on for the next week. Note any prayer requests from meeting.
1. _____	1. _____
2. _____	2. _____
3. _____	3. _____

Prayer for Accountability Partner:

Father, I pray for courage to be honest, humble, and transparent with the person you are placing in my life to hold me accountable to You. May we both be committed to covering every facet of our lives in prayer (Philippians 4:6-7).

WEEK 3

D∗I∗V∗A∗S Desires
Discovering Your Passion

Day 1 • Small Steps
Donna

> Each one of us has a purpose in the Lord. But many of us don't realize that.
> And when we don't have an accurate understanding of our identity, we either
> strive to be like someone else or something we're not. We compare ourselves
> to others and feel as though we always fall short. When we don't become
> who we think we're supposed to be, it makes us critical of ourselves and
> our lives. It causes us to be insecure, oversensitive, judgmental, frustrated,
> and unfulfilled. We become self-absorbed, constantly having to think about
> ourselves and what we should be. It forces us to try too hard to make life
> happen the way we think it is suppose to. In the extreme, it makes us tell lies
> about ourselves and become dishonest about who we really are. When you
> are around people who don't have any idea of what they are called to do,
> you sense their unrest, unfulfillment, anxiety, and lack of peace.
>
> Stormie Omartian, *The Power of a Praying Woman*[7]

If you didn't see yourself somewhere in those lines, take another look. This
paragraph sums up the majority of the problems women face.

Each of us has a purpose. However, many of us live our day-to-day lives
without any actions to help us fulfill our purpose. We know God has a plan
for us, yet we still choose to make things happen our way, and we don't
participate in the small steps to help us discover our purposes. Ladies, we must

not forget God *"has saved us and called us with a holy calling, not according to our works, but according to His own purpose and grace which was given to us in Christ Jesus before time began"* (2 Timothy 1:9). Your purpose is not some vast mystery that God delights in keeping from you. Actually, your purpose will become very obvious to you when you are faithful in your walk, faithful in the small things. The small things **are**:

- **Priorities:** *Seek first the kingdom of God and His righteousness, and all these things shall be added to you.* Matthew 6:33

- **Bible Study:** *Your Word I have hidden in my heart, that I might not sin against You.* Psalm 119:11

- **Prayer:** *Rejoice always, pray without ceasing, in everything give thanks; for this is the will of God in Christ Jesus for you.* 1 Thessalonians 5:16-18

- **Unconditional Love:** *The second is like it: 'You shall love your neighbor as yourself.'* Matthew 22:39

- **Accountability:** *Admonish the young women to love their husbands, to love their children, to be discreet, chaste, homemakers, good, obedient to their own husbands, that the Word of God may not be blasphemed.* Titus 2:4-5

- **Witnessing:** *Go therefore and make disciples of all the nations, baptizing them in the name of the Father, and of the Son and of the Holy Spirit.* Matthew 28:19

When we are connected to God by taking these steps, our purpose and our predetermined destiny become very clear. Unfortunately, most of us end up being unfulfilled, oversensitive, judgmental, frustrated, and insecure because we want God to give us the plan before we agree to participate. We want to skip the small items of faithfulness and jump right to the big plan.

These small steps seem so insignificant we don't bother to participate in them. Our thoughts go something like this:

- "Okay God, when you tell me what is going on, then I'll know how to pray."

- "Okay God, when I know which direction you're sending me, I'll know which Bible study to begin working on."

- "Okay God, when you're ready to use me, let me know. Then I'll start changing my attitude, my schedule, my finances, and my relationships. I'm just not ready to work on these things until I know it's worth it."

- "Okay God, I'm ready to do whatever you want me to; just wait until I finish my big project at work."

What "Okay God," deal have you offered recently?

_____

_____

_____

_____

_____

_____

In the meantime, we just make choices and decisions in our life based on who we convince ourselves we are and where we think we're going. We try hard to make life happen the way we expect it to, or the way that we think makes the most sense. When we do this, we forfeit living out our true purpose with joy and contentment, because when we do it our way, we can only make decisions based on what we know or think is in our future.

WEEK 3 • D*I*V*A*S DESIRES

We take away the supernatural power of an all-knowing God who wrote the master plan for our life long before we even had the ability to think.

He knows exactly how your life intricately weaves itself into a beautiful story that brings Him ultimate glory here on earth. Why would you even try to do it any other way?

Many of us want to do God's will; the problem is, many of us don't want to do our part. So why does God ask us to do so much before we get the big picture? It is a simple answer. If you aren't faithful in the small steps of your walk, you can't handle the bigger plan for your life. If you aren't where you need to be spiritually (daily participating in the small steps), then you can't fight/stand against the wiles of the devil and the principalities of darkness (Ephesians 6:11-12). You cannot accomplish your God-given plan and destiny until you are totally dependent on the Author of the plan.

Are you tired of the lies you're telling yourself?

Are you tired of trying to be someone you're not?

Are you tired of being unfulfilled, insecure, judgmental, frustrated, self-absorbed, critical of yourself, oversensitive?

Are you tired of a life of anxiety?

Are you ready for a life more abundant with purpose and passion?

Are you ready to do your part and participate in the small steps?

Devoted

Review Matthew 6:33, Psalm 119:11, 1 Thessalonians 5:16-18, Matthew 22:39, Titus 2:4-5, Matthew 28:19. These scriptures from the beginning of the devotion focus on several of the "small steps" we should be taking every day in our walk.

Individual

Next to each small step write one way you can make improvements in your life. For example, Prayer: I need to pray daily. I need to pray with more purpose.

Priorities:

_____

Prayer:

_____

Bible Study:

_____

Unconditional Love:

_____

Accountability:

_____

Witnessing:

_____

Via - Prayer

Write a prayer asking God to help you make these changes a priority in your day-to-day schedule.

_____

_____

_____

_____

_____

_____

DAY 2 • Defining Your Roles
Donna

We have listed six steps we must take in order to discover our purpose — our unique place in this world. One of the six steps is defining your roles and prioritizing your life around those roles. This also helps you see patterns of the roles you have played throughout your life, as well as seeing roles that you excel in.

List as many roles as you can that apply to you at this point in your life. (child of God, mother, sister, employee, wife, victim, roommate, teacher, mentor, cook, taxi driver)

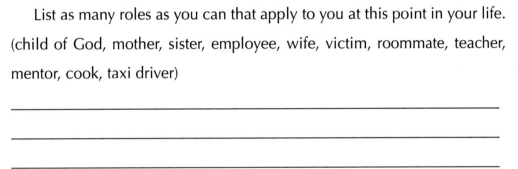

No wonder we're so good at multitasking!

These roles (relationships) take on many different forms. Some are easy roles that come naturally, and some are daily struggles. Some, such as a mother, sister, and daughter, are permanent and never-changing. Some, such as friend, accountability partner, and teacher, are choices. Some roles, such as caregiver, role model, survivor of a crisis, are demanded of us even if we don't want the responsibility.

It's important to examine which roles come naturally and which roles we excel in. These particular roles become guides, goals, or bench markers to help us find our true purpose in life.

Looking back at your life, is there a particular role that you continue to find yourself in, or that you enjoy or excel in? If so, list it on the lines below.

Steps to Discover Your Purpose

- Define your roles in life.
- Look at your character.
- Define your values and beliefs.
- Assessing your spiritual gifts and natural talents.
- Looking at your past.
- Discovering your passion.

The roles we play are important in helping us discover our purpose; but there are several occasions when our roles can hinder us from discovering what God has called us to do. By nature, (God designed us) we are nurturers and helpers. Eve was created to be a helpmate to Adam, to complement the attributes of man. (Sorry ladies, they've got strength and stamina and we've got mood swings and hormones.) As women, we tend to be so good at nurturing and taking care of others that we often overextend our relationship abilities to one of two extremes.

The first extreme is the woman who is responsible for so many roles in her day-to-day life that she cannot be committed to any of them. This can be used as a defense mechanism to keep relationships at a distance, but more often it is a case of trying to be superwoman. You know the type. The woman who is a wife, best friend, daughter, best friend, caretaker, best friend, employee, best friend, Sunday School teacher, best friend, and Red Cross volunteer. Just writing this all down was exhausting. This woman is spread so thin she can barely keep up with which role she's supposed to focus on. She ends up having surface level relationships with everyone, including God.

Can you relate to this extreme? Do you wear too many hats (roles)?

The next extreme is the woman who is so consumed by one role that she loses interest in all others. For example, a few years ago, I was home with my two small children both under the age of three. I was Mommy and nothing else. My energy and focus revolved around the needs of my children: eating, sleeping, changing diapers, and potty training. They consumed all of me. By the end of the day, my role as Mommy left no room for my role as wife, daughter, friend, or child of God. I was in serious, sleep-deprived survival mode, and all the energy I could muster went straight to my kids. Many of you who have children can relate. But there are other examples. For instance, the career that drains all your energy and allows no room for any other role. Another example is an unhealthy relationship with someone who is "high maintenance."

We all know women at both extremes, and probably have been both of these women at some point in our lives. Both extremes are unhealthy. They leave you feeling exhausted, unfulfilled, and empty. You become a person who is just going through the necessary emotions required by the role of the moment. You become a person without purpose or passion.

Are you just role playing?

When I was so caught up in my role as mother, I neglected my husband, my friends, and my relationship with God. My identity became my children. They were the only thing I could carry on a conversation about — the first tooth, the first word, the disastrous potty training episodes. (It was really evident when, on a rare outing with my sister, I asked the waitress where the "potty" was located.) These topics weren't bad; they were just all I was capable of discussing. Why? Because I had neglected all other roles in my life. After three years of this, I realized I was exhausted and miserable. Through my misery and a very good small group class at church, I realized my roles were not prioritized according to God's plan.

Thankfully, I had a strong marriage. After putting the needs of my husband over the needs of my children (not easy, but biblical), our marriage not only recovered but exploded with a new-found joy and passion. It took me longer to place my role as a child of God in the right slot of my priorities, but when I did, I had a renewed purpose and passion. It was and still is life more abundant. I see myself — and live daily — first as a child of God, second as a loving helpmate to my husband, and third as a nurturing, caring mother. It is a blessing to know and experience the peace and calmness in every role I am called to be because I am first a precious, unique child of God with a divine purpose. So are you!

God created us to be all of these roles. He gave us a guide to help us keep each in its rightful place in our day-to-day lives. We can only be **ALL** of these roles if we are **ALL** His first.

You can't be a good or even an okay wife, daughter, sister, friend, employee, teacher, or mentor, if you aren't first a devoted child of God. In order to find and live out your purpose in life, you have to master the priority list of the roles in which you are called.

A word of caution: This is one of the biggest traps of the devil because he definitely offers many other ways to prioritize, and they're often justifiable according to worldly standards and practices.

List three roles that are most important to you. Next, list one action for each role that you desire to accomplish or change in the next year.

*

Ephesians 1:11-12

In Him also we have obtained an inheritance, being predestined according to the purpose of Him who works all things according to the counsel of His will, that we who first trusted in Christ should be to the praise of His glory.

Ephesians 2:10

For we are His workmanship, created in Christ Jesus for good works, which God prepared beforehand that we should walk in them.

2 Timothy 1:9

Who has saved us and called us with a holy calling, not according to our works, but according to His own purpose and grace which was given to us in Christ Jesus before time began.

1. Role: _____

   Desired Action: _____

2. Role: _____

   Desired Action: _____

3. Role: _____

   Desired Action: _____

Devoted

Read the scriptures in the margin and circle the words that relate to your purpose in life.

Individual

Describe what you feel your purpose is in life.

_____

_____

_____

_____

_____

Via – Prayer

Write a prayer asking God to help you discover your purpose, your mission, in life as you continue this class.

_____

_____

_____

_____

_____

_____

_____

* * *

DAY 3 • Self Assessment

Donna & Sherri

The following exercise is a self assessment to encourage you to stop and think about yourself. Too often, life is busy and we rarely take time to think about what really is important to us. These questions might seem hard at first glance, but we encourage you to give each question some deep thought as you answer. Please understand there is no right or wrong answer. These questions reveal how little we know our true self and the motives behind what we do every day.

1. List three current goals you have in your life.

   a. _____

   b. _____

   c. _____

2. Define worship as it pertains to you.

   _____

   _____

   _____

3. What do you feel your "job" is here on earth?

   _____

   _____

   _____

4. What brings you a sense of contentment/peace in your busy schedule?

   _____

   _____

   _____

5. Why do you get up in the morning? (check all that apply)

   ___ a. Because I have to go to work.

   ___ b. My children are hungry.

   ___ c. I have to take the kids to school.

   ___ d. I just can't sleep anymore.

   ___ e. I really don't know.

   ___ f. It's just what I have always done.

   ___ g. _____

6. List three things you enjoy doing. (Anything that you can spend hours doing and lose track of time.)

   a. _____

   b. _____

   c. _____

7. On a scale of 1 to 100, rate the following areas of your life.
   (1 being the worst it could be and 100 being exceptional.)

   ___ a. Relationship with God   ___ f. Financial Position

   ___ b. Marriage   ___ g. Church Service

   ___ c. Relationship with Children   ___ h. Prayer Life

   ___ d. Friendships   ___ i. Family Relationships

   ___ e. Business/Job   ___ j. Physical Health

Devoted

Read 2 Timothy 2:19-22.

Individual

What insights have you learned from today's scripture or from the self assessment?

_____

_____

_____

_____

_____

_____

_____

Via – Prayer

Write a prayer asking God to use you for His divine purpose.

_____

_____

_____

_____

_____

_____

_____

_____

2 Timothy 2:19-22
God's truth stands firm like a foundation stone with this inscription: "The LORD knows those who are his," and "Those who claim they belong to the Lord must turn away from all wickedness." In a wealthy home some utensils are made of gold and silver, and some are made of wood and clay. The expensive utensils are used for special occasions, and the cheap ones are for the everyday use. If you keep yourself pure, you will be a utensil God can use for his purpose. Your life will be clean, and you will be ready for the Master to use you for every good work. Run from anything that stimulates youthful lust. Follow anything that makes you want to do right. Pursue faith and love and peace, and enjoy the companionship of those who call on the Lord with pure hearts. (NLT)

Day 4 • Self Assessment (Part 2)
Donna & Sherri

Complete the following questions. Remember, there are no wrong answers. These questions will help you to continue to uncover areas of passion and purpose in your life.

1. What three qualities do you want associated with your reputation?

   a. _____   b. _____   c. _____

2. List ten strengths you have.

   a. _____   f. _____

   b. _____   g. _____

   c. _____   h. _____

   d. _____   i. _____

   e. _____   j. _____

3. List six things that you are most proud of accomplishing.

   a. _____   d. _____

   b. _____   e. _____

   c. _____   f. _____

4. What three things have you been told you are good at? (decorating, cooking, time management, leadership, working with children, etc.)

   a. _____   b. _____   c. _____

5. List three character "flaws." (aggressive, angry, controlling, irresponsible, jealous, prideful, unreliable, etc.)

   a. _____   b. _____   c. _____

6. List eight things you would not want to live without. (friendships, to-do list, rewards, goals, recognition, commitment, safety, computer, etc.)

   a. _____   e. _____

   b. _____   f. _____

   c. _____   g. _____

   d. _____   h. _____

7. Fill in the next eight blanks by finishing this statement. "I believe in ...."
(Jesus, God, constitution, marriage, working hard, determination, etc.)

a. _____   e. _____

b. _____   f. _____

c. _____   g. _____

d. _____   h. _____

Devoted

Read Genesis 24:12, Proverbs 19:21.

Individual

What insights about your purpose have you gained from this assessment?

_____

_____

_____

_____

_____

Via - Prayer

Make Genesis 24:12 your prayer for today. Ask God to make you successful in His purpose for you.

_____

_____

_____

_____

_____

_____

Genesis 24:12

Then he said, "O LORD, God of my master Abraham, please give me success this day ...

Proverb 19:21

There are many plans in a man's heart, Nevertheless the LORD's counsel — that will stand.

Day 5 • A Gift For You
Donna

You cannot determine your purpose, your unique ministry, your unique act of worship, until you take into consideration the tools you have been given to accomplish your purpose. Your most important tool is your spiritual gift. It is the compass on your map. It will always give you a true sense of direction if you know how to use it. For this devotion we are relying heavily on Scripture to answer the questions about spiritual gifts. This is the "supernatural" part of your purpose, so we are going to let the Word of God speak for itself because *"it is living and powerful, and sharper than a two-edged sword, piercing even to the division of soul and spirit"* (Hebrew 4:12).

Here is what Scripture says:

- If you are a believer in Christ, you have a gift.

- Your gift was selected for you by the Holy Spirit to work for His purpose and His glory.

- Gifts are spiritual capacities that God gives to individual Christians.

- Believers' gifts will complement each other, just as the parts of the body complement each other and work together.

- Gifts can be used in many different avenues, but all come from the same Holy Spirit.

- Spiritual gifts are given for a three-fold purpose:

  1. For the equipping of the saints for the work of ministry.

  2. For the edifying (building up) of the body of Christ.

  3. To bring unity of the faith and of the knowledge of the Son of God.

- You are called to use your gifts to minister to others, as a good steward of the manifold grace of God.

- God supplies the "ability" behind the gift — this is how He is glorified. (In other words, it is not up to you to make it work. You just have to daily surrender yourself to God's will in your life.)

- You don't get to choose your gift — the Holy Spirit gives it as He wills.

We all have traits and characteristics that resemble the gifts. However, a gift goes beyond the average person's natural abilities, and can't be explained in any other way except as a special anointing of the Holy Spirit.

In David Francis' book, *Spiritual Gifts*, he defines a spiritual gift as a "God-given assignment, capacity, and desire to perform a function within the body of Christ with supernatural joy, energy, and effectiveness."[8] (I don't know about you but I'm up for supernatural joy and energy at any time!) Francis goes on to further explain this definition. Let's take a closer look so we can get a clear understanding of spiritual gifts.

- **God-Given Assignment** — This is not a choice! God created you for a specific job, a specific responsibility here on this earth.

- **Capacity** — You are capable of developing and growing within the realm of your gift.

- **Desire** — It really is a matter of a "want to," not a "have to" attitude when you start serving in the area of your spiritual gift. This is a great self-check question for each of us as we begin to serve in the church. For example, when I first joined my church, I started helping in the two-year-old classes one Sunday each month. I signed up because there was a need and my son was in the class. Every month when it was my turn, I dreaded going to church. There was no "want to" attitude about the two-year-old class. After I stepped down from this position, I started teaching the first D*I*V*A*S class. I loved it! I was excited to go. I was there early. I always had a "want to" desire to go to this class. So, if you are serving in a certain area but without that "want to" desire, this may not be where you are gifted. Find a different area of service and see if it brings you to a new level of excitement and desire to serve. If not, keep trying different areas until you discover the "want to" attitude.

- **To perform a function within the body of Christ with supernatural joy, energy and effectiveness** — The supernatural is the part of the gift that the Holy Spirit supplies. The joy, energy, and effectiveness really cannot be explained in any other manner. You will be blessed beyond words. You will be given the energy and effectiveness to complete whatever task pertains to your spiritual gift. Here is an example to help put this into perspective: One of the pastors at our church is a puppeteer. He planned, organized, created, and directed a full-scale Christmas Puppet Show. It was awesome, to say the least. It had black lights, singing camels, dancing stars, confetti guns and it all took place on a very elaborate stage that had four different scene areas. It was a wonderful production. I sat in my seat at the end of the show and realized that our pastor had put this together in a four week time frame, and still maintained the responsibilities of his job and his family. I remember thinking, "How did he do all of this?" If you were to ask my pastor that same question he would answer, "I can only explain it in one way—I didn't do it. God did it through me!" You see ladies, that is the supernatural part of the gift. If you are serving within your spiritual gift people will be asking you, "How do you do that?" You won't be able to answer this question in any other way except to say, "I didn't do it. God did!"

To further your knowledge of your personal spiritual gift, complete the gifts inventory you received in class. (A Spiritual Gifts Inventory can be downloaded from several resources, including at www.lifeway.com. There, search "Discovering and Using Our Spiritual Gifts." In this article midway down, click and print Spiritual Gifts Survey/Discovery Tool). The Spiritual Gifts Survey will help you discover potential gifted areas. This is a very good tool, but it doesn't take into consideration your life experiences and your environment. It is a guide. The only way you will be successful in determining your personal ministry gift is by continually seeking God's guidance through prayer and Bible study. Your gift is a blessing. It should express itself as a complement, as a tool, as a strength to allow your unique purpose in the body of Christ to be fulfilled.

Devoted

Read Romans 12:3-8, Ephesians 4:7-16, 1 Corinthians 12:4-11, 1 Peter 4:10-11. Circle your spiritual gift in the list below.

Administration	Faith	Mercy
Apostleship	Giving	Prophecy
Discernment	Hospitality	Service/Helps
Evangelism	Knowledge	Shepherding
Exhortation	Leadership	Wisdom

Individual

What insights have you gained from these scriptures on spiritual gifts?

_____

_____

_____

_____

_____

_____

_____

Via - Prayer

Ask God to reveal ways you can use your spiritual gifts to serve Him.

_____

_____

_____

_____

_____

Accountability

ACCOUNTABILITY PARTNER'S INFORMATION:

NAME: _____

PHONE: _____

         (home)   (cell)   (work)

EMAIL: _____

CONTACT DATE AND TIME: _____

Friendship Question:

Describe your favorite Christmas, birthday, or anniversary gift.

Accountability Questions:

Did you complete your D*I*V*A*S devotionals this week?

What "small step" do you want to improve? How are you going to make that change? (Day 1)

Spiritual Growth

I will continue my spiritual growth this week by completing the following action(s):

1. _____

2. _____

3. _____

List items your partner(s) will be focusing on for the next week. Note any prayer requests from meeting.

1. _____

2. _____

3. _____

Prayer for Accountability Partner:

Father, as I continue to seek your purpose in my life please send me a godly woman who will hold me accountable to the changes that are necessary in my life for spiritual growth. O God, establish a strong relationship as we share our strengths and weaknesses. May we encourage and support each other through the truth of Your Holy Word. (Ecclesiastes 4:9-12)

WEEK 4

D*I*V*A*S Dilemma

LIVING FOR THE FUTURE, NOT IN THE PAST
Donna & Sherri

This week we will begin working through the biggest dilemma facing all D*I*V*A*S. Your past!

We'll spend some time reflecting on the many ways your past has had an influence on who you are, your current behaviors, your belief system, your thought patterns. You'll be surprised at how much of your past you can remember. This will be very enlightening, empowering and humbling all at the same time. As your past unfolds, you'll discover the many people, events, truths, and illusions that have influenced you. Some of the events may be a joy to reflect on; some however may not be so joyous.

This week you will make a Life Map. As you draw, color, cut, and paste it together, it will represent your life as a whole. This activity will help you discover significant times and themes of your life. Don't rush this part of the exercise. Take time to really think about your life from the earliest moments. Try not to censor your thoughts and feelings as you complete your life map. Instead respect it all for what it is: the clay out of which your unique identity has been sculpted. From our experience, this activity has been the most helpful and eye-opening for other D*I*V*A*S. We encourage you to fully invest yourself in this process. You will have time to complete your map in place of devotions on Day 3 and Day 4.

First, begin by completing a **D*I*V*A*S Diary** of your past. List as much information as you can in each section on the following pages. It might help to look at your life in stages or to break it down into years. The more information you have on your map the better understanding you will have about your life. This is for your eyes only, so don't hold back. You won't be asked to share anything you don't want to share. Some things might be tough to put on paper, but trust in this process and allow yourself to see your past through new eyes.

People

Think of all your relationships with family members, friends, teachers, any one that had an influence on you (positive or negative). Think about fictional characters from books, heroes, role models. Include enemies and rivals as well.

Personal Events and Experiences

List your most powerful memories, crises, and crossroads. The happiest day of your life. Your most embarrassing moment. Personal victories, personal defeats, high times, low times. Your hardest decisions, your deepest hurts, your biggest accomplishments. Times of intense emotions: love, anger, hate, forgiveness, bitterness, compassion, grief, loss, fears you have faced, insecurities. This is an important step. Really look at your life as a whole. It may help to think of your life in stages or yearly increments. (K-5th Grade, Junior High, College, etc.)

Cultural World Events

Events that impacted the world you are a part of. Things that you believed in or stood for. (Vietnam, 9-11)

Significant Roles

Times when you were a hero, a victim, a friend, an outsider, caregiver. Which did you enjoy or hate? Which roles were comfortable? Which were overwhelming? Which roles will you have in your future?

Miracles, Answered Prayer, Words/Advice or Scripture that Impacted Your Life

After you complete the **D∗I∗V∗A∗S Diary** exercises read the following guidelines to help you construct your map.

1. Think about all the different kinds of maps. Which reflects your life the best: a garden diagram (with different types of paths)? road map (with many intersections)? an amusement park (with different attractions that resemble different stages of your life)? a floor plan of a house? a game board?

2. Next, reflect on the path that your life has taken. Has it gone in a circle? Where does it start — at the bottom, the right side, or in the middle? Does your map have sharp curves where life took a dramatic turn? Maybe it has dead ends or paths you could have taken but didn't. Does your map have circles, where you keep going through the same events/trials over and over again? Don't make this part hard just go with what you feel "fits."

3. Think about the symbol you will use to depict your life path itself: a line, broken line, foot prints, questions marks, rocks. Will your symbol change colors to show changing moods or times of growth/pain?

4. After you've decided what your life map looks like, review your **D∗I∗V∗A∗S Diary** information. Fill in as many influences as possible on your map by giving each one a symbolic place along your path. It might help if you create a legend and use similar symbols to identify and describe the meaning of life events.

5. You might also want to designate certain times of your life by giving areas of your map symbolic names such as: Forest of Fear, Whirlwind of Confusion, Tornado Alley (for times of loss/destruction).

For some women, looking back at their past is easy. For others, it is a scary thing to do. We encourage you to pray as you work through these exercises. If, at any point, you realize you need to talk with someone about circumstances in your past, we encourage you to speak with your facilitator or pastor to help you get closure, peace, and healing.

We've included two examples of life maps from other D*I*V*A*S. The first is a combination of symbols that represent different times/events/people in her life. Notice the way the little caterpillar at the bottom left corner transforms into the beautiful butterfly at the top. This woman really understood how God has used her journey to transform her into the beautiful person she is today. The second is very different in the way the woman used a garden path as the theme. Notice the different ways the path changes to represent the transitional times in her life. She used several different items, butterflies, rocks, and flowers, as her symbols. Be creative. You can also use pictures from clip art, the internet, or stickers to represent items on your map. It can be as simple or complex as you want to make it. We just ask that it means something to you!

DAY 1 • Prosperous Plan
Donna

"I know the plans that I have for you," declares the LORD, "plans to prosper you and not to harm you, plans to give you hope and a future. Then you will call upon me and come and pray to me, and I will listen to you. You will seek me and find me, when you seek me with all your heart. I will be found by you," declares the LORD, "and I will bring you back from captivity...."

Jeremiah 29:11-14 NIV

This is the theme, the underlying purpose, of everything we are trying to accomplish this week. Let's take a closer look at these verses and see how they relate to your purpose, your plan, your mission.

"I know the plans that I have for you," declares the LORD...

God knows His plan for you. You were created by Him for a unique purpose in His eternal plan. If you are reading this and breathing, then you have a reason, a destination, a purpose, a plan for your existence. Your heavenly Father, the Almighty Creator, the King of kings, the Lord of lords, has a plan for you!

Another translation states it this way: *I know the thoughts that I think toward you, says the LORD* (NKJV). God thinks about you. Not just a little bit, not just when you do good things, and not just when you do bad things. His thoughts of you cannot be numbered, for they are greater than the grains of sand. (Psalm 40:5)

How many times during any given day do you have thoughts about your spouse or children? Why do you think about them so much? Because you love them, you worry about their wellbeing, and they are an active part of your life. They are important to you. Sister, God loves you. You are important to Him. His thoughts about you cannot be numbered!

Plans to prosper you and not to harm you...

God is a loving Father who wants to shower you with blessings both earthly and eternal. His thoughts for you are of peace and hope. Peace in every situation. Peace to know He is in control. Peace to know there is a greater purpose and plan for your hurt, heartaches, struggles, trials, and pain. Peace that surpasses all understanding. God is not capable of evil. That is not in His plan for you. Yes, He will mold you and transform you to be more like Him. He does this through your trials and tribulations. The bad/evil in your life comes not from God, but from Satan. God wants to give you life more abundant. (John 10:10) But that doesn't mean you don't have to "pick up your cross" and carry it up a steep hill every now and then. You have to believe God's ultimate plan for your life is to prosper you — to give you something greater. Take this truth and live it out in your life. God's plan is a plan of peace and hope.

To give you hope and a future...

Yes, as a child of God you have an eternal future in God's presence. He also has a future for the rest of your earthly days. Remember, there was a reason, a purpose, that made Him think about you and form you perfectly for this earthly purpose. A future of hope — a hope for what you do not see so you can eagerly wait for it with perseverance. (Romans 8:24)

Then you will call upon me...

Here is your part, your responsibility. You must call upon God. You must choose to seek Him, to know Him. This is the only way you will know His wonderful plan for your life. Are you calling upon God?

And come and pray to me...

Prayer. Remember, prayer is a heavenly discussion — one in which you listen more than you speak. Prayer is developing your relationship through conversations and quality time. First, you call upon Him. Second, you pray to Him. (Philippians 4:6-7)

And I will listen to you...

Sister, you are that important to Him. The Almighty Creator of the heavens and the earth, the very Being who spoke Heaven and Earth into existence will listen to you. What you say to Him matters. Every minute detail of your life is important to Him, so He will listen to you.

You will seek me...

You will desire and delight in knowing Him. You will search for Him passionately. Why? Because He created you to seek Him. It's part of His plan.

Have you ever wondered why one of the most universal desires in the human race is to find a purpose, a reason to live? That's how we are all created — with a knowledge of who God is and a desire to fulfill that purpose for which we are created.

You will find me...

What a promise! What a comfort! What peace! You seek Him and you will find Him!

When you seek me with all your heart...

In other words, when you "take up your cross" — count the cost — and surrender your all to Him, every aspect of your heart is surrendered to God. Your whole heart has no room for earthly idols or desires. If you are empty of yourself, you can only be filled by Him.

I will be found by you and I will bring you back from your captivity.

God will deliver you from your captivity. He will set you free from whatever stronghold or burden is keeping you from His plan in your life. That is His promise to you. You do your part, and He will keep His promise to you. Are you willing to do your part? Are you willing to take up your cross? Are you willing to seek Him? Pray to Him? Call upon Him?

God is ready and waiting to fulfill His promise to you! Remember, He loves you so much He can't stop thinking about you.

Devoted

Read Jeremiah 29:11-14 again.

Individual

What plans do you think God has in store for your future?

_____

_____

_____

_____

_____

_____

Via - Prayer

Write a prayer asking God to reveal His plans to you. Ask Him to show you how to seek Him with all your heart.

_____

_____

_____

_____

_____

_____

Day 2 • Why Go There?
Donna

Why is looking at your past important to your future? There are several reasons for digging up the past at this point. We'll look at each reason throughout the next few devotions. We strongly encourage you to pray that God will open your eyes so you can see your past from a fresh viewpoint. Pray that the events of your past will help you discover who you are today. You must pray believing that God wants to redeem and restore what has been lost, hurt, or broken in your past. Also pray believing that He can take *anything* from your past and turn it into one of your greatest blessings today. He will weave it into the very foundation of your unique ministry. He will use it for His glory if you will surrender it to Him.

First, your past is what made you who you are today. No question about it — the events and experiences (good and bad) had some type of influence on the person you are today. This sounds like common sense to most of us, however, not many of us have ever taken the time to examine our past to see how it has influenced our behaviors and beliefs today.

As you completed your **D*I*V*A*S Diary** pages, I am sure you listed memories you have not thought about in a long time. Some of them were probably pleasant and brought a chuckle or a smile to your face as you recalled them. There may have been great memories about your first kiss, your first love, your first child, your best friend, your favorite vacation. There are probably also some not-so-good memories that you might have chosen to forget about because they're too painful. They bring back feelings of hurt, anger, brokenness, loss, shame. We tend to handle these memories in one of two ways. We surrender them to God and let Him restore and redeem us from the pain, or we hide the pain and never move forward. Whatever the memory, each experience impacted you in either a positive or negative way.

Oftentimes a memory's impact is so much a part of us that we don't even see it in our lives. For example, a woman who has been betrayed in the past by a friend or parental figure often has a hard time trusting another person in an intimate relationship. This lack of trust begins a spiraling cycle in that her life. She hesitates to open up in a relationship, for fear of being hurt again. Therefore, she struggles to connect with another person on a level that allows her to trust again. She ends up being betrayed again and again because she never trusted in the relationship, even when the other person deserved it. This inevitably leads to more betrayal.

Other experiences that have impacted our lives might not be so obvious. Yet, their impact on our behavior is undeniable. We often overlook these because they were more the result of an environment that we were a part of rather than a specific good or bad memory. We often learn behaviors we see around us. For example, if we grew up around critical or judgmental people, we have a tendency to weave those same characteristics into our own lives. Statistics show that if someone grew up around alcohol, drugs, or abuse (verbal or physical), that person is more likely to experience the same thing as an adult.

The same is also true for your marriage, the way you raise your kids, the way you interact with others. I have a hard time submitting to my husband because my mom has always been the spiritual leader in my family. It's very difficult for me not to step into my husband's spiritual sneakers...not because I don't trust him or don't want to submit, but more because I don't know how to do it any other way. This realization didn't come to me overnight. I, like you, have re-examined my past. I have done this exercise several times, and at different points in my life. I did it once in college, again several years ago through two different Bible studies, and more recently through my accountability relationship. I've prayed for God to give me fresh eyes and to reveal the "bad" from my past that I must surrender to Him to make "good."

One of the reasons you must examine your past is because it will help you understand the why's behind your actions today. We'll focus on your current behaviors and see if they relate to specific events in your life. A specific behavior can stem from several different experiences in your life.

Devoted

Read all of Ephesians 4:22-32. These scriptures are God's directions to you regarding your past.

Ephesians 4:22-24
That you put off, concerning your former conduct, the old man which grows corrupt according to the deceitful lusts, and be renewed in the spirit of your mind, and that you put on the new man which was created according to God, in true righteousness and holiness.

Individual

Ask yourself the following questions to gain insight on how your past has influenced your behavior and who you are today. What behaviors do your need to "put off"?

- Are you overly sensitive? Judgmental? Critical? Negative? Unforgiving? Bitter? Never satisfied?

- Do you have a tendency to mistrust people?

- Do you have an "I don't need anybody's help, I can do it myself" attitude? (By the way this is pride and it can be a stronghold. I know. It's one of mine.)

- Are you striving for perfection?

- Are you afraid of commitment?

- Do you over commit yourself?

- Do you have a need for control?

List any behaviors or characteristics you need to "put off."

_____

_____

_____

_____

_____

_____

Via - Prayer

Take some time to pray and really examine your behaviors and beliefs and see how they are related to your past experiences. Then, write a prayer surrendering your past experiences to God. Ask God to restore and redeem the hurt and pain. Pray for Him to reveal negative behaviors from your past that you may not be aware of so you can surrender them to Him. Ask Him to "renew your mind and put on the new woman."

Prayer of Surrender:

_____

_____

_____

_____

_____

_____

_____

_____

DAY 3 • Take Off the Old!
Donna & Sherri

Devoted

Take some time to work on your life map today. Continue to focus on patterns, behaviors, attitudes, or sinful ways that you need to change in your life. Read Ezekiel 18:31, Psalm 51:10, Romans 6:4, Colossians 3:1-10.

Individual

As you focus on your map today note what "new" things God reveals to you to "put on" in order to replace the "old." On the lines below, describe what your new heart looks like. Is it more forgiving, more trusting, more compassionate, free from lust, depression, anger?

_____

_____

_____

_____

_____

Via - Prayer

Spend some time today in prayer asking God to give you wisdom and courage to take off the old and put on the new in your life.

_____

_____

_____

_____

_____

_____

Ezekiel 18:31

Cast away from you all the transgression which you have committed, and get yourselves a new heart and a new spirit....

Psalm 51:10

Create in me a clean heart, O God, and renew a steadfast spirit within me.

Romans 6:4

We were therefore buried with him through baptism into death in order that, just as Christ was raised from the dead through the glory of the Father, we too may live a new life. (NIV)

Colossians 3:1, 5, 8-10

Since you have been raised to new life with Christ, set your sights on the realities of heaven....So put to death the sinful, earthly things lurking within you....But now is the time to get rid of anger, rage, malicious behavior....for you have stripped off your old evil nature and all its wicked deeds.... clothed yourself with a brant-new nature.... (NLT)

Day 4 • You – Healed
Donna & Sherri

Devoted

Circle the word brokenhearted in the verses in the sidebar. To be complete and new in Christ you must allow God to heal your pain and brokenness. We will cover more on this subject in Week 5. Today, take some time to focus on completing your life map for class.

Individual

Who can heal your brokenness and your pain?

_____

What will Jesus Christ give you instead of "ashes and mourning"?

_____

_____

What will you display as a result of letting Jesus Christ heal your pain?

_____

_____

Via – Prayer

Write a prayer asking God to replace the pain of your past with a garment of praise for Him. Ask Him to display His mighty power in your life, regardless of your current or past circumstances.

_____

_____

_____

_____

Psalm 34:18
The LORD is close to the brokenhearted. (NIV)

Psalm 147:3
He heals the brokenhearted and binds up their wounds.

Isaiah 61:1-3
The Spirit of the Lord GOD is upon Me, because the LORD has anointed Me to preach good tidings to the poor; He has sent Me to heal the brokenhearted, to proclaim liberty to the captives, and the opening of the prison to those who are bound; to proclaim the acceptable year of the LORD, and the day of vengeance of our God; to comfort all who mourn, to console those who mourn in Zion, to give them beauty for ashes, the oil of joy for mourning, the garment of praise for the spirit of heaviness; that they may be called trees of righteousness, the planting of the LORD that He may be glorified.

Day 5 • You – Complete
Donna & Sherri

As we close this week we hope you've seen your past through new eyes. We pray you realize that when you accept Jesus Christ as your Savior you then have the right, the privilege, and the responsibility to become a new creation — a new creation, that represents God's mercy and grace...and most important, His great love. Answer the following questions today as you continue to process your past. Realize the Almighty God of heaven and earth has always been in control of everything on your map. May you have a deeper understanding and peace about your past; peace that only comes from God. Our prayer is that God will reveal to you a renewed strength and a deep passion to use your life, the good and the bad, as a vessel to bring Him glory.

1. How did you feel completing your map?

   _____

   _____

2. What were the hardest things to put on your map?

   _____

   _____

3. What events/people in your past had you not thought about in a long time?

   _____

   _____

4. Do you see God's work in your map? Explain.

   _____

   _____

5. Are there areas of your life that you need closure on?

   _____

   _____

6. What or who has influenced you the most in your life?

   _____

   _____

7. Do you see any behavior patterns from your map?

8. Is there a trial/hardship/struggle you are thankful to have experienced?

9. What have you learned from your struggles?

10. What strengths have you gained from your battles?

11. Is there anything from your past you need to let go of today?

12. How can God use the "bad" or "hurtful" times from your past in your future?

13. Does your past bring clarity to your future? If yes, explain.

14. Did you discover an area of potential "ministry" from your map?

15. How can your past change your future?

Devoted

Read Genesis 50:15-20 and Romans 5:3-5. The words from Genesis are the words that Joseph said to his brothers — the very brothers who sold him into slavery and told their dad he had been killed by a wild animal.

Genesis 50:20

As for you, you meant evil against me; but God meant it for good, in order to bring it about as it is this day, to save many people alive.

Romans 5:3-5

Not only that... tribulation produces perseverance; and perseverance, character; and character, hope. Now hope does not disappoint, because the love of God has been poured out in our hearts by the Holy Spirit who was given to us.

Individual

After reflecting on your past this week, how has God used the bad things in your past for good? What hope do you have in your future?

_____

_____

_____

_____

_____

_____

_____

_____

_____

Via - Prayer

Write a prayer asking God to bring glory to His name through your life.

_____

_____

_____

_____

_____

Accountability

ACCOUNTABILITY PARTNER'S INFORMATION:

NAME: _____

PHONE: _____

             (home)   (cell)   (work)

EMAIL: _____

CONTACT DATE AND TIME: _____

Friendship Question:

Describe one of your favorite childhood memories.

Accountability Questions:

Did you complete your D*I*V*A*S devotionals this week?

What is one behavior or characteristic (good or bad) that comes from your past?

Spiritual Growth

I will continue my spiritual growth this week by completing the following action(s):	List items your partner(s) will be focusing on for the next week. Note any prayer requests from meeting.
1. _____	1. _____
2. _____	2. _____
3. _____	3. _____

Prayer for Accountability Partner:

Father, place in my path an accountability partner who can relate to my past and understand the changes that I need to make in my life. Father, give us both wisdom and discernment as we encourage and challenge each other in our daily walk with You. (Ephesians 4:32, Colossians 3:16)

WEEK 5

D∗I∗V∗A∗S DESIGN
THE MASTER'S PLAN FOR YOUR LIFE

DAY 1 • More Than Skin Deep
Donna

In 2007 I underwent a surgical procedure because I had some questionable issues with my breasts. Many of you can relate to this topic because it affects so many of us. Before the surgery, I went through the multiple mammograms, duct-o-grams, doctors' visits, radiological reports, and surgical consultations. This all took place in the span of about seven months before the final decision was to remove the questionable "tissue." I remember the day before the surgery. My dear accountability partner called to say a prayer with me over the phone. (An undeniable advantage of accountability is a true prayer partner.) We both were choked up by the moment. She said to me, "You know, Donna, no matter the outcome, God has a plan for this in your life. Who knows? This may be the next devotion you write." We laughed at the idea. That was the last I thought about that comment until I was standing in the shower a few minutes before I began writing this. (I do some of my best thinking in the shower.) Those seven months seemed to come full circle into some sense of a "learning experience," if you will.

Stay with me on this one.

You see, something had been wrong in my body. Nobody knew exactly what it was or why it had been causing these particular oddities to occur. Even after the routine test, examinations, lab work, surgical consults, we still had no conclusive evidence. Our next step was to surgically remove the suspect tissue so they could examine it through a microscope and run further tests to see if it was cancer related. The recovery process wasn't as bad as the doctors had predicted. (Thanks to many answered prayers for a pain free recovery, I didn't even need a pain pill.) After the results from the surgery came back, there was still no conclusive answer as to the cause of the problem. However, the tissue was declared benign and nothing triggered red flags about being at risk for cancer. Praise God!

About three weeks after the surgery, life had returned to normal, except for one thing. My body had started healing, and so had the nerves in the surgical area. Every now and then I felt stinging, shooting pains, like quick bee stings. It was uncomfortable for a moment, but not unbearable. I also noticed I was more sensitive at the surgical site. Even the water from the shower had become uncomfortable. (This is probably the reason everything came full circle in the shower!) I found myself instinctively jerking a hand up every time I turned into the stream of water. I kept trying to cover the area even, though I knew that in order to have a full recovery without infection or further complication I must wash the wound area.

So how do a breast, a surgery, and a shower fit into a devotion about your past? Here's my explanation: The "bad stuff" in my body was causing it to do unexplainable things that it should not do.

The "bad stuff" in your past could be causing you to do unexplainable, or even unnoticeable things in your day-to-day thought patterns, behaviors, and attitudes (as we discussed in the last devotion).

In my case, the experts (doctors, radiologist, and surgeons) couldn't explain the why or what that was causing my body to act this way.

Similarly, experts (friends, family, TV, self-help books) might not be able to explain the why or the what about your past. They might not even see the connection of your past to who you are today.

I allowed the experts to to remove the "bad" in order for their eyes to examine it through the lens of a microscope. They performed numerous scientific tests, the industry standard, in order to determine what the tissue was.

You also need to remove the "bad" in your life and examine it through the eyes of God. You also need to "test" your past against the industry standard of Biblical truth.

The doctors never came up with a definitive why or what; but they did conclude that it was benign (not cancerous...good).

You, too, may never know or understand the why or what that occurred in your past. But you are promised as a child of God that He will make it good! (Romans 8:28)

I still have occasional little stingers of pain. I will always have a scar at the wound site, even though my body has perfectly healed.

Even as you find closure and healing from your past you may still encounter some uncomfortable stingers of emotions from time to time. You may always bear a visible scar even after you have completely healed. These are reminders of the trials and "scary moments" in your life that you have overcome with God's grace and strength. (2 Corinthians 12:9)

I was tempted every time I took a shower to place my hand over the sensitive area to protect it from the very water that would cleanse it and ensure a full recovery.

In order for you to fully recover from your past you must uncover it, and wash it clean with the cleansing power of the living water of Jesus Christ. You must allow Him to redeem and restore you from the "bad" so that it becomes the "good" in your walk.

Devoted

Read Romans 8:28-39, 2 Corinthians 12:9-10.

Individual

What insights have you gained from these scriptures that will help you get through difficult circumstances?

_____

_____

_____

_____

_____

Via – Prayer

Take some time today to write a prayer surrendering "the bad." Ask God to reveal to you "the good" He has planned for you as you move forward. Ask Him to reveal the right procedures for dealing with your past. Pray about the "experts" you may need to consult with regarding your past.

_____

_____

_____

_____

_____

_____

Romans 8:28

We know that in all things God works for the good of those who love him, who have been called according to his purpose. NIV

2 Corinthians 12:9-10

My gracious favor is all you need. My power works best in your weakness." So, now I am glad to boast about my weakness, so that the power of Christ may work through me. Since I know it is all for Christ's good, I am quite content with my weaknesses and with insults, hardships, persecutions, and calamities. For when I am weak, then I am strong.

DAY 2 • Forgiveness

Donna

A bee. This symbol on my life map represented the hurt and betrayal from an individual in my past. I am sure you've added several "bees" as you've been working on your map. You might manifest or represent it in your life differently, but it's the one thing we have in common. Everyone has hurt, betrayal, anger, disappointment, and pain on her map. Some of us might have bigger bites and deeper wounds than others; some of the bites might be buried deep in our past; some might still be fresh and stinging.

We live in a fallen world. That means we live with people who are not perfect (even though some people are convinced they are). The Bible tells us all have sinned and fallen short of the glory of God. We have all hurt others and been hurt by others. My mother would say, "That's just life, deal with it." She was right. We must deal with it! So how do we deal with it the D*I*V*A*S way? We look to the great example that Jesus set before us. How do we deal with it? Forgiveness!

Forgiveness is another term we Christians use a lot; but we rarely practice it or live it out the way Jesus taught us in the Bible. It is defined in Vines Dictionary[9] as "to release from all debts," or "to bestow a favor unconditionally."

Forgiveness. Is it a feeling or a choice? We need to examine several misconceptions about forgiveness. What is it, really? And how do we do it? To find the answers, let us first begin by looking at what forgiveness is *not*, followed by the example that Christ gave us to follow.

- **Forgiveness is not a feeling. You will never willingly want to forgive the person who inflicted hurt or pain in your life.**

Forgiveness is a choice. In fact, before His death to forgive our sins, Jesus went to His Father in the garden and asked Him if there was any other way to accomplish this great act of forgiveness. He prayed, "Father, if it is Your will, take this cup from Me; nevertheless not My will but Yours be done." (Luke 22:42) Jesus chose to die for you. His Father in heaven, Almighty God, your Father, chose to let His son die for your sins.

To add a little earthly perspective on this divine act of forgiveness and love, imagine you have the same choice. Many of you are mothers, god-mothers, or aunts. You love your precious children. There is nothing like holding a newborn baby in your arms. It is an instantaneous love, a love that is indescribable until you experience it. As a mother, you would do anything to protect your children from being hurt. Often when they are sick or hurting you even wish and pray that you could switch places with them so they don't have to experience hurt and pain.

Now think of the worst villain imaginable. Get a vivid picture of what this person has done to hurt children and families. Then imagine yourself sitting at the trial of this person. The judge and jury have declared this criminal guilty beyond any shadow of a doubt and sentenced this heartless person to death. As the criminal actually smiles at this conviction, the judge turns to you and says, "However, I will spare this person from death — in fact, I will set all criminals free — if you will give your child as a substitute. Will you allow your child to suffer mentally, physically, and ultimately die a horrifying death by crucifixion in place of this criminal's death sentence?"

Just the thought of that sends cold chills down my spine. No way would my human mind allow these criminals to have "a get-out-of-jail-free card" at the expense of any of my precious children's lives. Yet God did just that. He sent his only son to be tortured, betrayed, beaten, and hung on a cross for every sin that was and will ever be committed. Was it a feeling? Did either God or Jesus "feel" like doing it? No! It was a choice! It was an act of love! It was an act of forgiveness!

- **Forgiveness is not ignoring a wrong; in fact, it is acknowledging the wrong.**

Jesus knew firsthand the sting of betrayal. Did He just pretend that it didn't happen? Did He just "forget" the fact that the very disciples He had invested so much of Himself in had completely denied their relationships and betrayed Him? No. He acknowledged the wrong. Luke 22:34 tells us that before Peter was even in a position to deny knowing Him, Jesus told Peter it would happen: *He (Jesus) said, "I tell you, Peter, the rooster shall not crow this day before you will deny three times that you know Me."*

We must acknowledge the hurt, pain, and/or betrayal in order to be able to forgive it. This is hard to do when the very people we love are the ones who have caused us the deepest hurt. We tend to make excuses for the wrongs we have experienced. We tell ourselves, that it is our own fault, or the wrong really isn't that bad, ot it must be just a little misunderstanding. In some cases, such as molestation, rape, and/or adultery, we even go so far as to completely block out the memory altogether because the pain is too difficult to endure. But, in order to forgive we must acknowledge the wrong (sin) and accept that it happened. That is what Jesus did.

- **Forgiveness is not forgetting the wrong. Instead, it is allowing God to give you a new perspective of the wrong and use this new perspective to represent His love in your life.**

The biggest misconception about forgiving is coined in the phrase "forgive it and forget it." This, my friend, is not humanly possible. You'll always know you were hurt and/or betrayed. Just because you forgive the person doesn't mean you forget. I don't believe God wants us to forget it; if He did He wouldn't have written the Gospels! The story of Jesus forgiving us and dying for our sins is a testimony of God's love for everyone. It's the very reason we shouldn't "forget." When we forgive a person, we aren't forgetting the hurt; instead, we're choosing to love regardless of the hurt. We're choosing to allow God to use the hurt in a divine way, through us, to minister to others. One of the best ways to share the love of Jesus is to forgive the person who has hurt you and to allow God to love that person through you anyway. Not because you forget the hurt, but because He loves, despite the hurt. Therefore, you love despite the hurt.

- **Forgiveness is not an act between you and another person. Forgiveness is an act between you and God. Reconciliation is the act between you and another person, after forgiveness has taken place between you and God.**

Often, people mistakenly think of forgiveness as an act between two people. However it is not. Reconciliation is the act of making peace with another person.

People are also often under the impression that reconciliation must take place before they can forgive. This is not true. You can forgive regardless of whether or not the relationship between you and the person who hurt you is ever reconciled. The other person may never be sorry for what they did, yet you can still forgive them, because forgiveness takes place between you and God.

If you are a child of God, you have confessed your sins to God and asked Him to forgive you. You have reconciled the relationship. You can do this because Jesus paid the price for your sins when He died for you. You can reconcile the relationship because you were first forgiven. While Jesus was on the cross he said, *"Father, forgive them, for they do not know what they do."* (Luke 23:34) This was a conversation between Jesus and His Father. In the same way, when you forgive someone, it is a conversation between you and God.

Forgiveness is necessary for you to have a relationship with Christ. Scripture reveals to us the importance of receiving forgiveness in order to be forgiven. In Ephesians 4:31-32 we read, *"Let all bitterness, wrath, anger, clamor, and evil speaking be put away from you, with all malice. And be kind to one another, tenderhearted, forgiving one another, even as God in Christ forgave you."* As you look at your life map and reflect on your past you must acknowledge the pain, the hurt, and/or the betrayal to God. You must release all of your bitterness, wrath, anger, clamor, and evil words toward the person. You must forgive the person who sinned against you. God wants to redeem this pain, hurt, or betrayal into a testimony of His love in your life. This is part of your ministry.

Forgiveness isn't easy! This is obvious even, when Jesus was in the act of forgiving the entire world. Luke 22:44 states: *Being in agony, He prayed more earnestly. Then His sweat became like great drops of blood falling down to the ground.* Luke 22:43 tells us even God in heaven knew this was a difficult task; He sent an angel to strengthen Jesus. Sister, forgiveness may be hard for you, but rest assured Jesus understands what you are facing. You must also believe God will strengthen you!

Today as you continue to reflect on your past, we encourage you to do two things Jesus did. First, He prayed for strength. Second, He surrounded Himself with others (the disciples) to pray for Him.

Devoted

Read Romans 3:22-24, Luke 23:34, Ephesians 4:31-32.

Individual

What insights, instructions, or inspirations do you feel God is saying to you regarding forgiveness?

_____

_____

_____

_____

Write the names of two people that you will ask to pray for you as you begin the act of forgiveness.

NAMES OF PRAYER PARTNERS:

1. _____

2. _____

Romans 3:22-24

This righteousness from God comes through faith in Jesus Christ to all who believe. There is no difference, for all have sinned and fall short of the glory of God, and are justified freely by his grace through the redemption that came by Christ Jesus. (NIV)

Luke 23:34

Jesus said, "Father, forgive them for they do not know what they are doing."

Ephesians 4:31-32

Get rid of all bitterness, rage and anger, brawling and slander, along with every form of malice. Be kind and compassionate to one another, forgiving each other, just as in Christ God forgave you. (NIV)

Write the names of people you need to forgive:

_____

_____

_____

_____

Via – Prayer

On the lines below, write a prayer asking God to strengthen you and to help you forgive the people you have listed above the way He forgives you.

_____

_____

_____

_____

_____

* * *

Day 3 • A Forgiving Heart

Sherri

Yesterday we confirmed that forgiveness is not always easy, but it is something God requires of us. The word *forgive* appears over 140 times in the New Testament. The definition of the Greek word used for *forgive* includes "to let go," "to leave behind," "to dismiss," and even "to cancel a debt." It is used for forgiveness of sins by God (implying also the canceling of guilt).

If *forgive* is used 140 times, then it appears that forgiveness is something of great importance to God. We must have a forgiving heart even though we will not always forget the pain that was caused. God's love is amazing. Regardless of how many times we disappoint Him, His big heart never fails to beat with unconditional love for us. Only through a relationship with Jesus can we find true forgiveness in our hearts for those people who have hurt us in the past and the people who will hurt us in the future.

Devoted

We are called to live a life that represents the love of Christ. Read the following verses and circle the characteristics that should be evident in our lives even toward those who have wronged us.

Psalm 103:8-14

The LORD is compassionate and gracious, slow to anger, abounding in love. He will not always accuse, nor will he harbor his anger forever; he does not treat us as our sins deserve or repay us according to our iniquities. For as high as the heavens are above the earth, so great is his love for those who fear him; as far as the east is from the west, so far has he removed our transgressions from us. As a father has compassion on his children, so the LORD has compassion on those who fear him; for he knows how we are formed, he remembers that we are dust (NIV).

Matthew 6:14-15

If you forgive men when they sin against you, your heavenly Father will also forgive you. But if you do not forgive men their sins, your Father will not forgive your sins (NIV).

Individual

What insights, instructions, or inspirations do you feel God is saying to you about forgiveness? How will forgiveness give you freedom from your past? How will forgiveness strengthen your relationship with Jesus Christ?

_____

_____

_____

Via – Prayer

Take some time today to reflect on the forgiveness that you received from Jesus' death on the cross. If you have never experienced the loving forgiveness that is yours because of Jesus dying on the cross for your sins, then make that commitment right now. The following is a short prayer asking Jesus into your heart to forgive you and to make Him Lord of your life.

Dear Heavenly Father,

On this day, I admit I am a sinner and was born a sinner. I know and believe the Scriptures as they describe Your great love for me as You sent Your one and only Son to die on the cross for my sins. I believe that on the third day He arose and conquered death so that I will one day live in heaven with You. Father, on this day I want to ask You into my heart and make You Lord over my life.

Amen.

If you just prayed this prayer for the first time please share this with your class leader or a pastor.

Write a letter to Jesus thanking Him for what He did for you.

_____

_____

_____

_____

_____

_____

_____

_____

_____

_____

_____

Day 4 • Jesus Within
Donna

As we seek to grow into all that God has called us to be we must take a closer look at the relationship we have with the Holy Spirit — the Jesus within.

Most of us have encountered the Jesus within, when the Holy Spirit knocked on our heart's door and asked to come in (Revelation 3:20). We each opened the door and felt the true power of the Holy Spirit as our sins were forgiven and we were made new in Him (2 Corinthians 5:17). This conversion is usually a moment that every child of God can describe in great detail because it can be such a real, life-changing experience. Often we bask in this spiritual moment for several days. For those of us who have been really "big" sinners according to the worldly hierarchy of sin we might live in this moment for a month or two longer.

Before long this Jesus within us just becomes part of who we are in the flesh. This becomes a mere feeling that we tap into during brief "God moments" in our lives — such as a powerful message preached to us from a pulpit or a touching song sung at a women's conference. It is a mere tug at the heart here and there in our lives. In these really intense moments we feel a touch of the true power of the Jesus within. Really, think about it. Most of us feel closeness to God during brief moments characterized by hardships, sickness, death, births, and even weddings. For some of us who attend church regularly or perhaps listen to Christian radio, our brief "God moments" may be more frequent simply because we are exposing ourselves to opportunities to stand in the shadow of a Jesus who lives in others. Regardless of how often the encounters are, one thing is true for the majority of us. Momentary brief encounters with the Jesus within dot the path of our lives and form the basis of our relationship with Jesus Christ.

Stop and reflect for a moment on just how many God-moments you have experienced in the last seven days. Write them down in the margin.

Many of us consider ourselves modern-day disciples. We walk in the shadows of Jesus by going to church on Sunday, and offering up brief prayers for improved health or financial gain. We might even shout out a few praises of thanksgiving during those brief "God moments" we experience throughout life. We learn a little about Jesus here and there from speakers, songs, and preachers. The "really strong" disciples, might even look up a scripture or two every now and then for clarification about the lesson in Small Group or Sunday School. Overall, the carnal nature of who we are today is not a whole lot different than who we used to be before Jesus within. Neither were the disciples! Surprised? Me too. This statement caught me off guard when I read it in Joanna Weaver's book, *Having a Mary Spirit: Allowing God to Change Us from the Inside Out.* Here is how she explained her statement.

> These 12 handpicked men had left their families and livelihoods to follow Christ. Yet after being privy to all the inner workings of God on earth, after enjoying front-row seats to hundreds of miracles never seen before by the human eye, they still doubted Jesus when they faced impossibilities like really big storms, really bad demons, and really hungry people. Even as Jesus walked toward Jerusalem and the Cross, His disciples were still arguing about who would be greatest in the kingdom that they were certain He came to build. They were just as clueless at the end of Christ's time on Earth as they were at the beginning of His ministry.[10]

This sounds like most modern-day Christians' "Jesus experiences!" We are just as clueless as the disciples were at that point in their walk. They knew Jesus. They not only walked with Him in person, they ate with Him, prayed with Him, lived with Him. You can't be much closer to a person than the disciples were to Jesus when He was here on this earth. So, what happened that changed the disciples, that created a world-wide Christian movement from just 12 people? Jesus left us as a physical body and sent each one of His children a helper, a spirit to live within us. He breathed down the essence of who He is into the very being of the disciples (John 20:22). He did the same with you and me the day we opened the door and accepted Him as our Savior. So, why are our lives more representative of the disciples lives when they were walking and learning in the shadows of Jesus than the disciples lives after they received the Holy Spirit — the Jesus within?

Let me share with you what I think is part of the problem.

- **We look to see Jesus in others instead of searching for Jesus within ourselves.**

  We never stop to realize the essence of the Holy Spirit in us as our comforter (Acts 9:31), our guide (1 Corinthians 2:13), our helper (John 14:26), and our hope (Romans 15:13). In other words, we bask in the glow of great sermons or speakers because we see Jesus alive and working in their lives. Yet, we are not willing to make a personal commitment to get to know the Jesus within ourselves through prayer and Bible study.

- **We become numb to the presence of the Holy Spirit because of sin.**

  We quench the Holy Spirit's power because we hang on to bitterness, anger, jealously, unforgiveness, unkind words or thoughts, and negative attitudes (Ephesians 4:30). We become deaf to the voice of Jesus within; therefore, we continue living life our way instead of following the example Jesus set for us.

- **We don't die to ourselves and let Jesus shine through us (1 Corinthians 6:19).**

  We are so proud to be who we are and what we want to that we never release control of our carnal wants, "needs," desires and dreams.

  We must surrender every aspect of our lives to the complete authority of Jesus Christ. We must daily seek the power of Jesus within us through prayer and His Word. We must daily confess and cleanse our hearts of sin and of our wants and desires so the Jesus within us can shine through. Only then will we become disciples who have the power to change the world around us. Only then will we experience a "God moment" in every moment.

Devoted

Read Acts Chapter 2 and imagine what it must have been like for the early Church to see Jesus alive on this earth in his physical body, then to experience firsthand the "pouring out" of the Holy Spirit — the Jesus within — in their own lives after his death and resurrection. What an indescribable experience it must have been! Do you feel the Holy Spirit poured out in your life?

Individual

What did you learn about the Holy Spirit in this chapter? Do you experience the Holy Spirit every day in your life? Is the Jesus within you evident to the lost world around you?

_____

_____

_____

_____

_____

Via – Prayer

Write a prayer of commitment to God expressing your desire and willingness to deepen your relationship with Him through your prayer time and Bible study.

_____

_____

_____

_____

DAY 5 • Goliath and the Chirping Bird

Sherri

I was shocked! I was actually scared! I began to back away, but the bird continued to come after me. He had jumped from the ledge to the floor, determined to protect himself from the giant obstacle — me. As he continued running toward me, I quickly backed in circles around a very large coffee table trying to avoid the horrible "pecking" I knew I was about to receive.

Moments later, as I gained my sanity, I started laughing at myself and the ridiculous episode that had just occurred. A five-foot three-inch young adult running from a four-inch, beady-eyed bird?

As I was catching my breath I looked over my shoulder to see if anyone had witnessed this little bird escapade. Were my "cool points" forever gone?

I couldn't believe it. Just a few minutes earlier on this beautiful, sunny day I'd been calmly completing my college intern homework assignment. It had been during this calm that I'd first noticed the tiny black bird serenely chirping away on the ledge in front of me....

I welcomed break from the stress of college to just enjoy nature — peaceful nature. So, I decided to be a little adventurous and see how close I could get to the little bird.

As began to inch my way toward it, I could tell it had taken a sudden interest in me, too, because we locked gazes.

He was curious. I was curious.

I took a few more steps...closer, closer...until I froze in amazement. The tiny little bird wasn't moving, as I'd expected it would. I knew it was scared by the louder, not-so-peaceful chirping it was now making. My nurturing side thought, "The poor bird must be hurt; it isn't flying away! His chirping's getting louder and louder! He must be in excruciating pain! I need to help him!"

I's taken a few more steps toward the bird when it happened.

That little bird wasn't hurt. Oh no! He was perfectly healthy! Perfectly determined to stand his ground, too!

That had been the big day for the little bird; he'd decided in that very moment he would face his fears. It was a David and Goliath battle in his tiny, pea-sized brain, I'm sure. Fear or no fear he'd been determined to stand his ground and guard his territory. So off that ledge he'd flown, sending Goliath Sherri running around a table, gasping for air, and heart racing. That had been his day. His day of change!

That little bird had his day (at my expense of course) but he had faced his fears – Goliath Sherri. He had taken the necessary steps, or rather the necessary leap off the balcony, to change his fear into a positive experience and a better life. I on the other hand, had let the fear of a tiny bird make me run in circles, gasping for air, not seeing the big, overall picture. Fear had blocked my vision (and my common sense) of the simple steps necessary to rid myself of this tiny creature. — Stop running and say, "Shooo!"

I look back on this through tears of laughter, now, and realize that fear of even the tiniest of things can be a stumbling block to our accomplishments. Fear is one of the main reasons people don't change. We're afraid to step out of our comfort zone. I realized from this funny episode that we must take control of our personal situations and we, ourselves, must be the catalyst to change our outcomes in life. We must view change in a positive light! (That little bird certainly did!)

As we reach this section of our journey together you've discovered many areas that you might desire to change. You've taken a self-assessment to discover areas you like or dislike. You've prioritized your most important roles. You've completed a spiritual gift inventory to discover the unique gifts God has given to you. You've examined your past for thought patterns and belief systems that you might need to change. You've offered forgiveness to those who have hurt you. Each these items has brought you to a point where you desire to change certain areas of your life or your future.

We have the ability to choose change. So, how is it that most of us run in circles in life instead of embracing change...something different? We become comfortable in our current situations, good or bad, therefore we don't want to move out of our comfort zone. We're afraid of the unknown. God tells us many times to "fear not." Why? Because He gives us the strength and courage to face our fears. He gives us the ability to make choices and to do so with a positive attitude. He requires that we trust Him and have faith in His plan for us. When thinking about change, we have to realize and accept that it begins with me and you. With God's help, we are the only ones who can change our circumstances.

Think about accepting Jesus. Doesn't this require change? It requires changing our old ways, our old habits and learning to live with a more Christ-like attitude. God requires us to become child-like in our ways so that we are open to change — open to learning and growing in Him. Even though this can be hard at times, God's Word tells us that we *can do all things through Christ who strengthens* us (Philippians 4:13). If this is so, then why should we fear change? God is telling us that He gives us what we need to be able to get through any situation. He only requires that we trust Him.

As you continue in this study you'll be focusing on making positive change a reality in your life. This will require making decisions about what you're truly committed to in life. It will require making some changes in the way you've always done things. It might require changing some relationships. It could mean giving up some things that you once thought were necessary. It might mean creating some new habits that will seem difficult at first.

We're all familiar with the cliché, "If you aren't growing, you're dying." To me, this simply means that if I am doing the same thing the same way I've always done "it" — whatever "it" is — nothing will ever change. "It" will always be the same. Doesn't that sound boring? How exciting will life really be if we are not creating something new for ourselves?

Why is change important? Because God requires us to change so that we are continually growing into the person He has designed us to be. In D*I*V*A*S terms, change means spiritual growth!

Devoted

Read Acts 3:19-20 and Isaiah 1:16-20. This is God's Word, His plea to you today. Will you commit to change? Will you move out of your comfort zone? Will you be obedient? Will you commit to live life the way He has called you to live it? God promises you in these verses, that if you obey you will be satisfied!!

You've spent the last two weeks looking at your past. Now it is time to close that door and start living as the new creation God can make you — as pure as fresh fallen snow! You have a choice at this point in your life. Just as the little bird faced his fears, you too can take this next step — for some of us, like the little bird, it is a leap — of faith into the new that God has in store for you!

Individual

What changes do you feel God is asking you to make in your life? Think about all you have learned about yourself, your patterns, your behaviors, your roles, your priorities, your past, your new ministry, your new hope in Christ, your new strength in Christ. Now take some time to list all the areas that you feel you need to change in your life. Don't hold back. Use this time to get it all on paper.

_____

_____

_____

_____

_____

• Look back over your list of desired changes and circle the ones that relate to spiritual growth.

Acts 3:19-20
Now turn from your sins and turn to God, so you can be cleansed of your sins. Then wonderful times of refreshment will come from the presence of the Lord… (NLT)

Isaiah 1:16-20
Wash yourselves and be clean! Let me no longer see your evil deeds. Give up your wicked ways. Learn to do good. Seek justice. Help the oppressed. Defend the orphan. Fight for the rights of widows. "Come now, let us argue this out," says the LORD. "No matter how deep the stain of your sins, I can remove it. I can make you as clean as freshly fallen snow. Even if you are stained as red as crimson, I can make you as white as wool. If you will only obey me and let me help you, then you will have plenty to eat. But if you keep turning away and refusing to listen, you will be destroyed by your enemies. I, the LORD, have spoken!" (NLT)

- Look over your list again and draw a box around any areas that relate to your marriage.

- If you are a parent, underline areas that relate to your children.

- If you are not married or if you do not have children, draw a box around your second area of priority (family, career, health, finance, etc.)

- Underline your third priority.

Via - Prayer

Write a prayer asking God to give you the courage and trust to step out of your comfort zone so that you can make the changes necessary to grow and deepen your relationship with Him. Ask Him to give you wisdom over the next few weeks as you take practical steps to implement these changes in your life. Praise Him for sending His Son so you have this opportunity to change and become a new creation!!

_____

_____

_____

_____

_____

_____

_____

Accountability

ACCOUNTABILITY PARTNER'S INFORMATION:

NAME: _____

PHONE: _____
          (home)   (cell)   (work)

EMAIL: _____

CONTACT DATE AND TIME: _____

Friendship Question:

Describe one of your personal "chirping bird and Goliath" experiences.

Accountability Questions:

Did you complete your D*I*V*A*S devotionals this week?

What steps have you taken this week toward forgiving someone on your list? (DAY 2)

Spiritual Growth

I will continue my spiritual growth this week by completing the following action(s):

1. _____

2. _____

3. _____

List items your partner(s) will be focusing on for the next week. Note any prayer requests from meeting.

1. _____

2. _____

3. _____

Prayer for Accountability Partner:
Father, I pray for my phone call accountability partner this week. Give her a spirit of forgiveness regarding the names she listed on DAY 2. Help her let go of any bitterness and anger that she is harboring. Give her the peace and kindness to forgive these people who have hurt her so that you can redeem her pain. (Ephesians 4:30-32)

WEEK 6

D•I•V•A•S DISCIPLINES
TOOLS FOR BALANCE AND JOY

DAY 1 • GOAL Is Not Another Four-Letter Word
Donna

Are you a goal-oriented person?

When I ask people if they're goal-oriented, I find their reaction and responses quite humorous. I, myself, have not always seen the humor in the word *goal*, nor was I fond of writing goals. (I'll explain more about this dislike in a moment.) However, I know my life was been turned upside down with the simple process of writing goals.

I am also surprised at the number of people who find the process of little importance. My husband is one of them! But I must admit after he has seen the changes it has made in my life, his interest has peaked. He is not a true believer in the process yet, but has been willing to adapt some of the principles into his life. (Honestly, I think it is more of the "I'll prove you wrong" approach but, hey, I'll take what I can get!)

I haven't always been a goal-oriented person; a person who wrote down goals and tried really hard to meet them. I was probably more like the majority of people. I had plans of going to college to find a successful career. I had plans of getting married one day and having children. I had plans of buying a house and owning a vehicle. Pretty standard plans but not really "goals."

In fact, my impression (ultimate dislike) of writing goals stemmed from my college courses. I have a degree in Recreational Therapy, but any of you who have worked in the health care industry probably have a similar background in writing goals. For an entire semester (hence the dislike) I was taught the way to write a measurable goal. I learned that a goal has three parts: actions that can be measured, criteria in which the action takes place, and a time frame in which these actions must be met. I spent hours making up goals for potential patients. I was drilled on the importance of writing goals in this fashion in order to meet the standards of hospitals and insurance companies; these goals must also be written in order to justify the patients' improvement or non-improvement. Naturally, as I entered the working world, I discovered that every facility taught its own (and different) way to write important goals. Not all facilities required the all-important three-parts, and each facility had completely different standards regarding what was an appropriate goal. Nonetheless, the one thing they all shared was the fact that writing goals is the way to measure the patient's progress and be reimbursed.

As I left my career field, I never saw the importance of writing goals again. After all, I didn't need to monitor my ability to walk 50 feet, nor my ability to carry on a conversation without saying anything suicidal (both common patient goals in my field).

Then along came this person into my life who has always been very goal oriented, very A-B-C and 1-2-3 about her life. She had mapped out a Life Purpose Statement and listed five goals that were important to her. Now she was asking me to hold her accountable to her very own goals. Yes, at first, I thought she was a little excessive about spending that much time writing down all of her goals and each step it was going to take her to get to each goal. I wasn't at all interested in doing that for myself. It seemed like a pointless waste of my time. I was a stay-at-home mom. I didn't have big goals at that point in my life; hey, I didn't even have a career. My focus really was providing the basic needs of my children. In other words, I made beds and peanut butter and jelly sandwiches. I played peek-a-boo and molded play dough. I thought to myself, "What would I write as a goal for myself? I can walk 50 feet and carry on a conversation without having suicidal thoughts, so what would be the point in writing goals? I don't have a career at this point and I'm basically functioning just fine." (I'll bet many of you feel the same way right now.)

However, I found my new friend's concept of writing personal goals intriguing. So I asked to read the book[11] that had inspired her desire for accountability with her goals. As I read this book, I was blown away by the statistics that proved the difference it makes in a person's life to write down goals and review them daily. According to those statistics, people who do this are largely more successful in all aspects of their lives. I started to realize that I am a person who is willing and wanting things to continually improve in my life. I want to continually build up my marriage and improve my parenting skills. I am a person who wants things to happen a certain way in my life, such as early retirement, debt freedom, ability to travel to different places. I want to be healthy and happy. I'm sure you are this person as well. You want certain things out of life. You want certain events to take place. You want to be a certain type of person, don't you? Surprise, you are goal oriented!

No, I didn't just trick you into that. It's just reality. There are two types of people: Those who never want to improve or change any aspect of their lives *or* those who want improvement and change. If you are the second type, then you are goal oriented, regardless of how you answered the question at the top of the page. (I was just as surprised as some of you at this realization.)

Here is the sobering fact: If you want change, then you must take certain steps to make that change happen. If you want change you have to be purposeful and accountable in taking those necessary steps in order to create this change. It won't happen without action on your part.

After reading the book, I gained a new perspective on goal setting. It does have a place in my life. (More than the 50-feet I can walk.) There is a place for it in your life, too. Throughout this study you may have discovered many areas of your life that you want to change or improve.

D*I*V*A*S realize that spiritual growth only occurs with change. We are providing you with a simple process in goal-writing and establishing accountability so you can meet these goals. All we ask is that you try this process for 90 days to see if it makes a difference in your life. We know it will. The statistics prove it!

So, I just want to ask you one last question… "Are you goal oriented?"

Your answer should be a resounding, "Yes!"

Devoted

Read Proverbs 16:1-4, 1 Samuel 18:14.

Individual

What do these verses say to you about success in your areas of change?

_____

_____

_____

_____

Via – Prayer

Write a prayer asking God to show you how to commit to His plans for you.

_____

_____

_____

_____

_____

_____

_____

_____

Proverbs 16:1-4
To man belong the plans of the heart, but from the LORD comes the reply of the tongue. All a man's ways seem innocent to him, but motives are weighed by the LORD. Commit to the LORD whatever you do, and your plans will succeed. The LORD works out everything for his own ends – even the wicked for a day of disaster. (NIV)

1 Samuel 18:14
In everything he did he had great success, because the LORD was with him. (NIV)

DAY 2 • Top 10 Reasons for Goal Setting

Sherri

10
Written goals strengthen your character by promoting a long-term perspective.

9
Written goals allow you to you lead your life as opposed to simply managing it.

8
Written goals provide internal, permanent, and consistent motivation.

7
Written goals help you stay focused — to concentrate on what's most important.

6
Written goals enhance your decision-making ability.

5
Written goals simultaneously require and build self-confidence.

4
Written goals help you create the future in advance.

3
Written goals help you control changes, to adjust your sails, to work with the wind, rather than against it.

2
Written goals heighten your awareness of opportunities that are consistent with your goals.

1
And finally, the Number One reason for writing your goals down: The most important benefit of setting effective goals is the person you become as a result of the pursuit!

(Information from *Success Is Not An Accident* by Tommy Newberry[12])

Okay ladies, goal oriented or not, let's "walk" through the process together. By this point in the study, through your quiet time, accountability phone calls, and class discussions you will have discovered some areas in your life you would like to change. By the time you complete this week's devotional you will have established practical ways to begin this process of change. As you know, true D*I*V*A*S understand and live out accountability and spiritual growth in their day-to-day lives...and spiritual growth only occurs with change!

1. Look back at Week 3 Day 2 and read over the Desired Action you want to accomplish or change in your top three roles.

2. Below, list what you want to accomplish or change in each of these roles. Make your statement specific. Don't answer "Why this is important?". We will come back to this later.

Role: (Spiritual)

Desired Action/Change: _____

Why is this important to me? _____

_____

Role: (Wife)

Desired Action/Change: _____

Why is this important to me? _____

_____

Role: (Mother)

Desired Action/Change: _____

Why is this important to me? _____

_____

3. Review your desired changes and reflect on the following questions.

    *   How would your accomplishment make you feel?

    *   What would it look like?

    *   How would this change inspire, motivate, and encourage you to step out of your comfort zone in order to accomplish something you didn't even think possible?

    *   What would your relationships in each of these roles look like if you made this change? Would they be deeper? Stronger? More fulfilling?

    *   Is there a particular subject you need to focus on in each role in order to accomplish this change? (Examples: prayer, forgiveness, peace, more investment in your marriage, encouraging parent, healthy lifestyle, prosperous living, positive attitude in work place)

4. Now go back and answer "Why is this important to me?". List two reasons you want to make this change in your life right now — what about this change makes it compelling enough to give you the desire to accomplish it. The following is a list of some examples:

Grow deeper in my walk	To change my lifestyle
I want to be obedient	I receive God's blessings
I want to heal my marriage	To experience marital bliss
Improve my marriage	I am committed to my vows
Increase family togetherness	I want to build strong family ties
To bond my new family	To invest time in my children
To live to see my grandchildren	

Devoted

Read 1 Chronicles 4:10, 2 Chronicles 26:5.

Individual

You might recognize the first of today's scripture verses as the prayer of Jabez. His brief prayer lets us know that he was a humble man who desired to be productive in accomplishing the plans and purpose that God had for his life. How will knowing God's plan for you in your three roles confirm your purpose and help you achieve your desired areas of change?

_____

_____

_____

_____

_____

_____

> **1 Chronicles 4:9-10**
> There was a man named Jabez....He was the one who prayed to the God of Israel, "Oh, that you would bless me and extend my territory! Please be with me in all that I do, and keep me from all trouble and pain!" And God granted him his request. (NLT)
>
> **2 Chronicles 26:5**
> He sought God during the days of Zechariah, who instructed him in the fear of God. As long as he sought the LORD, God gave him success. (NIV)

Via - Prayer

Write a prayer asking God to make sure your motives are right with your areas of change so you can be sure you are following His plan for you.

_____

_____

_____

_____

_____

_____

_____

DAY 3 • Effective Goals Are
Sherri

Written

Writing your goals in sentence form is the most important step in goal setting. Big dreams and wishes transform into goals through the act of actually being written! When you write your goals, you make them concrete, tangible, and physically real. A written goal helps you crystallize your thinking and gives you something to review so you can keep your goals in focus. Having your goals on paper increases your self-confidence. Being able to see what you have accomplished will give you a powerful sense of self-worth and will encourage you to set better and more challenging goals in the future. By putting your goals in writing you form an accountability contract with yourself.

Stated In Present Tense

Stating a goal in present tense communicates that goal to your brain in the most effective format, allowing you to clearly visualize your goals and start to really believe it is possible to accomplish. For example: "I accomplish... I build... I have..." instead of "I will...."

Stated Positively

Words are symbols for thoughts and ideas. Each time you write or say a word, you evoke a vision in your mind, so it's important to avoid stating or writing your goals in a negative way. Example: "I eat healthy, nutritious foods" instead of, "I will no longer eat junk food."

Consistent With Your Life-Purpose Statement

Your goals should cause you to become more like the person you were created to be. They should be personally meaningful. Effective goals are best established after you thoroughly think through your life and compose your Life Purpose Statement. Connect each goal to a particular value or role in your life. There should be a deep and obvious connection between your goals and your Life Purpose Statement.

Specific and Measurable

There must be no fuzziness in the statement of your goal. A goal must be measurable so that you or someone else can objectively evaluate your progress and determine exactly when you have achieved the goal, or if a new course of action should be taken. The more specific your goal, the clearer you will be about what steps to take. The more focused you are on your goal, the more you'll be aware of the people, ideas, and resources around you that can help you reach that goal.

Time Bound

Make sure your goals have reasonable deadlines for accomplishment. It's just human nature to put things off. Deadlines will put positive pressure on you to take action.

Reasonable and Challenging

Your goals should cause you to stretch, grow, and get out of your comfort zone. You should set goals that are achievable, but also build character by requiring you to exercise your self-discipline and perseverance. In order to fully develop your potential, you must be willing to experience some discomfort. Some experts suggest goals should have a 50-50 probability of success.

Thoroughly Planned

Have tangible action steps for each of your goals. Compile the details, make a plan, write out all of the activities, prioritize them, time organize them, and rewrite them as often as possible to make your plans reality. Revise it, improve it, plan it, and think it through on paper.

(Adapted from *Success Is Not An Accident*, by Tommy Newberry[13])

Examples of Different One-Year Goal Statements

Spiritual

- I am a prayerful servant who has a deeper friendship with God by spending quality time with Him each day.
- I am an obedient servant of God exemplifying strong spiritual maturity in the following areas: prayer, time in the Word, tithing, fellowship.
- I have a deeper understanding of faith and obedience.
- I deepen my relationship with God through a more intimate prayer life.

Wife

- I intensify our relationship by my positive words, physical touch, simple gifts, increased quality time, and acts of service.
- I am a forgiving wife who is committed to building our marriage through kindness, compassion, humility, and patience (Colossians 3:12).
- I am a wife who is submissive and supports my husband with a gentle and quiet spirit.
- I strengthen my marriage by becoming a wife after God's own heart.

Mother/Grandmother

- I teach my children biblical principles through consistent family quiet time.
- I have a close relationship with my children through structured activities.
- I make our mixed family a single family unit through structured activities.
- I have a balanced family schedule that incorporates each child's interest with quality family time.
- I am on guard and available to my children through purposeful prayers and weekly communication with them.

Now we're going to turn your areas of desired change/accomplishment (from yesterday's devotion) into written statements that will become your goals for the next 12 months. These examples will help you convert your desired changes into measureable goals. When you write your goals, make bold statements that will affirm your desired outcome. Write these statements in present tense sentence form as if they have already happened/been accomplished and as if you are already that person. For example: *I am* or *I have* statements. (Note how the example one year goal statements on the previous page are in sentence form.)

Role : Spiritual

One Year Goal: _____

_____

_____

Role : _____

One Year Goal: _____

_____

_____

Role : _____

One Year Goal: _____

_____

_____

Devoted

Read 1 Corinthians 9:24-27.

1 Corinthians 9:24-27

Do you not know that in a race all the runners run, but only one gets the prize? Run in such a way as to get the prize. Everyone who competes in the games goes into strict training. They do it to get a crown that will not last; but we do it to get a crown that will last forever. Therefore I do not run like a man running aimlessly; I do not fight like a man beating the air. No, I beat my body and make it my slave so that after I have preached to others, I myself will not be disqualified for the prize. (NIV)

Individual

What can you learn about goal setting ("running for the prize") from Paul?

_____

_____

_____

_____

_____

Via – Prayer

Write a prayer asking God to give you the faithfulness, the determination, the heart, the desire, the passion that is evident in Paul's life to run with purpose in pursuit of the eternal crown!

_____

_____

_____

_____

_____

_____

DAY 4 • Top Three

Sherri

Structure has always been a part of my life. Sometimes that has been great, and other times I've wished I could be more spontaneous and not have so much to do. More than I like to admit, many times I've been Martha (busy, busy, busy) when I wished I had been Mary (sitting at Jesus' feet for some quiet time with Him).

This was especially true several years ago. I had so many things on my plate that I couldn't focus and keep things in perspective. My boss kept telling me I was great at so many things, which was exactly why different organizations wanted me to head various committees.

I kept telling my husband I thought something was wrong with me medically, because I'd always been able to do 10 things at once, and do them well. Suddenly I was forgetting things and missing meetings, which is very unlike me. My husband said I just had too much on my plate.

I scheduled an appointment with my doctor, who confirmed that I was going through some anxiety and panic attacks due to stress. I scheduled an appointment with our pastor, who of course reconfirmed that I was going in so many different directions I couldn't hear God speaking to me.

I had heard the same message from my husband, my pastor, my boss, and my doctor, not to mention several close friends. Each had told me I was so busy I didn't even know who I was anymore. Finally, I realized I needed to re-focus on what was really important in my life. I needed to get some calm perspective back in my life. I had lost all sense of direction and purpose. This was the root of all of the stress, anxiety, and worry I had been experiencing. Even the physical symptoms were a result of the chaos in my life. Psalm 46:10 became my focus: *"Be still, and know that I am God."*

At this same time in my life, I was completing a program at work that required me to go through similar steps that we've been focusing on in this

D*I*V*A*S curriculum; I evaluated my strengths, my weaknesses, my dreams, and my future career. I was also completing a very challenging Beth Moore Bible study[14] that helped me examine my relationship with God, my past relationships, and my future. All of this helped me put some direction back into my life. I knew it was God's plan for me to focus more time on my spiritual growth and marriage. It was very challenging, but looking back I can see I needed to remove some community volunteer projects I was involved in so I could focus on the things that really mattered to me. Now, my life is more balanced. There are still times I feel like I move through my day like a whirlwind, but now that my focus and my personal goals are back in order, I can deal with these hectic and frenzied days in a much calmer and positive way.

During that time I was challenged to set some goals on paper and to establish an accountability person in my life to help me reach my goals. I focused on Romans 12:1 to help me get started: *"I urge you brothers, in view of God's mercy, to offer your bodies as living sacrifices, holy and pleasing to God — this is your spiritual act of worship"* (NIV).

We know our greatest desire should be to live lives of holy worship and devotion to God. This requires making sure that we don't conform to worldly ways and that we pursue God with passion and focus. We know God's intent is for us first to worship Him and make Him top priority in our life, second to focus on our spouse/family and third, to serve others.

I have since focused on my roles as a child of God and a spouse as my top two priorities. For my spiritual goal I chose to work toward a more effective prayer life with my spiritual accountability partner. I also established steps to improve my relationship with my husband (i.e. dedicate a weekend each month to just us — taking dance lessons, no plans with friends or family, etc.).

My mentor has always told me when I get rid of things I'm not passionate about, then I will excel at my real passion in life. This is the reason goal setting is so important — we must know what we are committed to in order to be able to say "No" to things that don't match up with our calling/purpose/ministry. My passion and ministry are now clear and easier to focus upon because I am taking daily steps to improve my most important roles.

You started this process on Day 1 by writing your 12-Month Goals. The next step in this process will teach you how to gain perspective on your purpose, simplify your life by refocusing your priorities. It will also offer simple steps to a more abundant life.

Take a few minutes and continue this process in your life by adding specific and measureable short-term goals. These goals will become your quarterly goals (90-Day Goals). Remember, each step is a small step toward accomplishing the spiritual growth and the change that you desire.

Look back at your 12-Month Goals on Day 3 and reflect on the following questions to help you write one specific item you can focus on for the next ninety days, in order to move you closer to accomplishing your 12-month goal.

- In what ways can you become more knowledgeable on this subject?

- Are there books you can read or classes you can take?

- Are there Bible stories or specific chapters/scriptures that apply?

- Can you increase your knowledge, learn a new skill, or focus on a consistent routine?

- What is one part of your goal that you want to focus on for the next quarter?

Now, take some time to write your 90-Day Goal for your three roles. Write your goal in present tense sentence form as a statement or affirmation. Again, we have included examples of 90-Day focus goals that would move a person closer to reaching one of the individual one-year goals listed in **Day 3**. Don't worry about the specific actions you need to do to make the 90-Day Goal happen. We'll cover that later.

Role: Spiritual

One-Year Goal Statement: (Sample)

- I am a prayerful servant who has a deeper friendship with God by spending quality time with Him each day.

4 Potential 90-Day Goals (Sample)

- I educate my self on the five principles of prayer – Praise, Confession, Petition, Intercession, Meditation.
- I establish consistent quiet time in my schedule.
- I use the D*I*V*A*S *Walk of Purpose Journal* to deepen my growth.
- I am knowledgeable on the subject of prayer.

Now it's your turn!

Copy your One-Year Goal Statement for your spiritual role onto the lines below. Next, write a statement in sentence form describing the one area you will be focusing on for the first quarter.

Role: Spiritual

One-Year Goal Statement: (from DAY 3)

_____

_____

_____

_____

90-Day Goal Statement:

_____

_____

_____

_____

Role: Wife (or your next priority if you are not married)

One-Year Goal Statement: (Sample)

• I intensify our relationship by my positive words, simple gifts, increased quality time, and acts of service.

4 Potential 90-Day Goals (Sample)

• I encourage my husband with positive words each week.

• I am my husband's playmate through planned quality activities.

• I give my spouse a small gift as a visual symbol of my love each week.

• I bring joy to my marriage through simple acts of service.

Now it's your turn!

Copy your One-Year Goal Statement for your second priority on the lines below. Next, write a statement in sentence form describing the one area you will be focusing on for the first quarter.

Role: _____

One-Year Goal Statement: (from DAY 3)

_____

_____

_____

_____

90-Day Goal Statement:

_____

_____

_____

_____

Role: Mother (or your next priority if you are not a mother)

One-Year Goal Statement: (Sample)

- I teach my children biblical principles through consistent family quiet time.

   4 Potential 90-Day Goals (Sample)

  - I creatively schedule family quiet time into our busy agenda.

  - We complete a children's Bible study on tithing.

  - We create a family prayer journal with personal prayer guides.

  - We share God's love with others during the holiday season by serving in our church and community.

Now it's your turn!

Copy your One-Year Goal Statement for your third priority on the lines below. Next, write a statement in sentence form describing the one area you will be focusing on for the first quarter.

Role: _____

One-Year Goal Statement: (from DAY 3)

_____

_____

_____

_____

90-Day Goal Statement:

_____

_____

_____

_____

Devoted

Read Psalm 37:3-6; 16:8-11; 145:19.

Individual

What insights have you gained from these scriptures that will give you confidence in writing and accomplishing your goals?

_____

_____

_____

_____

_____

Via - Prayer

Write a prayer asking God to show you how to commit to His plans for you.

_____

_____

_____

_____

_____

Psalm 37:3-6
Trust in the LORD, and do good; dwell in the land, and feed on His faithfulness. Delight yourself also in the LORD, and He shall give you the desires of your heart. Commit your way to the LORD, trust also in Him and He shall bring it to pass.

Psalm 16:8-11
I have set the LORD always before me. Because He is at my right hand, I will not be shaken. Therefore my heart is glad and my tongue rejoices; my body also will rest secure, because you will not abandon me to the grave, nor will you let your Holy One see decay. You have made known to me the path of life; you will fill me with joy in your presence, with eternal pleasures at your right hand. (NIV)

Psalm 145:19
He will fulfill the desire of those who fear Him; He also will hear their cry and save them.

Day 5 • 1-2-3 Action!
Donna & Sherri

The final stage of the goal-setting process is taking specific action steps necessary to accomplish your 90-Day Goals. These steps will be strategic action items that move you toward achievement of your 90-Day Goal in each role, which in turn, applies toward the success of your 12-Month Goal in each role. Some of these steps might be one-time items you need to accomplish. Some of these steps might be daily or several-times-a-week action items. It is not necessary to always have multiple action steps. You might simply need to take a class or read a book one quarter to gain the specific knowledge you need to be able to complete the 90-Day Goal. Then, there might be quarters when you will need to accomplish three to six items in order to achieve your 90-Day Goal. Each item should be tangible and easy to accomplish within a 90-day period. Complete the D-I-V section, then complete your action steps for your goals. We pray that as you read the scriptures from Paul, you are inspired to fully commit to your goals and the small steps that will make your goals a reality!

Devoted

The relentless pursuit of a goal was a passion for Paul! He wrote of pressing toward the goal for the prize (Philippians 3:14) and of running toward a prize and disciplining himself to "obtain" that prize (1 Corinthians 9:24-25). In both cases, however, Paul was running for an eternal goal, not an earthly trophy or treasure.

You have to believe that God wants you to be successful in all that you pursue. He simply calls you to align your goals toward right and eternal things. The D*I*V*A*S ultimate goal is for you to always please God by discovering His priorities; studying His principles; determining His plans for you; measuring success by His definition. He wants you to remember His promises of support, strength, guidance, and comfort.

Individual

In the folowing scriptures underline Paul's "lessons" about goal setting. We have underlined the first two for you. (There are 15 more.)

Philippians 3:12-21

I don't mean to say that I have already achieved these things or that I have already reached perfection! But <u>I keep working</u> toward that day when I will finally be all that Christ Jesus saved me for and wants me to be. No, dear brothers and sisters, <u>I am still not all I should be</u>, but I am focusing all my energies on this one thing: Forgetting the past and looking forward to what lies ahead, I strain to reach the end of the race and receive the prize for which God, through Christ Jesus, is calling us up to heaven.

I hope all of you who are mature Christians will agree on these things. If you disagree on some point, I believe God will make it plain to you. But we must be sure to obey the truth we have learned already.

Dear brothers and sisters, pattern your lives after mine, and learn from those who follow our example. For I have told you often before, and I say it again with tears in my eyes, that there are many whose conduct shows they are really enemies of the cross of Christ. Their future is eternal destruction. Their god is their appetite, they brag about shameful things, and all they think about is this life here on earth. But we are citizens of heaven, where the Lord Jesus Christ lives. And we are eagerly waiting for him to return as our Savior. He will take these weak mortal bodies of ours and change them into glorious bodies like his own, using the same mighty power that he will use to conquer everything, everywhere. (NLT)

I Corinthians 9:24-27

Remember that in a race everyone runs, but only one person gets the prize. You also must run in such a way that you will win. All athletes practice strict self-control. They do it to win a prize that will fade away, but we do it for an eternal prize. So I run straight to the goal with purpose in every step. I am not like a boxer who misses his punches. I discipline my body like an athlete, training it to do what it should. Otherwise, I fear that after preaching to others I myself might be disqualified. (NLT)

After reading the goals that Paul wanted to accomplish, which goal-setting lesson(s) do you see as most important to you in achieving your goals?

_____

_____

_____

_____

_____

Via – Prayer

Write a prayer asking God to show you how to make each action step purposeful so that you can accomplish your goals and be a living testimony to others around you.

_____

_____

_____

_____

_____

_____

_____

Lessons from Paul on Goal Setting

(Philippians 3:12-21, 1 Corinthians 9:24-27)

- I will keep working toward the prize.

- Christ Jesus saved me and wants me to be more.

- I will focus all my energies on this one thing.

- I will forget the past and seek what lies ahead.

- I strain, I push myself past my comfort zone.

- God will make it plain to me the direction I should take.

- I must obey the truth of God's Word which I already know.

- I will learn from other's who are strong examples.

- I will beware of the enemies of the cross for they focus on earthly rewards.

- My body is weak and mortal but God has the power to change me!

- I must run this race to win the ultimate prize.

- I will practice strict self control.

- I run straight toward my goal and do not waver.

- I make each step purposeful.

- I discipline my body and my mind to do what it should.

- I strive for the eternal riches!

- I must work hard to make my life a living testimony to the lost people around me.

Role: Spiritual

One Year Statement: (Sample)

• I am a prayerful servant who has a deeper friendship with God by spending quality time with Him each day.

90-Day Goal Statement (Sample)

• I educate my self on the five principles of prayer — Praise, Confession, Petition, Intercession, Meditation.

Potential Action Steps for 90-Day Goal Statement (Sample)

1. I buy Dr. Greg Frizzell's book *How to Develop a Powerful Prayer Life*.[15]
2. I have lunch with the prayer coordinator at church to ask questions I have about meditation.
3. I pray through the five principles of prayer during my quiet time.
4. I journal my intercessory prayers each week.
5. I set up a journal with five tabs for each principle.
6. I commit to focused prayer time each day.

Now it's your turn!

Look back at your 90-Day Goal Statement and write down simple actions that you will take in order to accomplish this goal.

Role: Spiritual

1. _____
2. _____
3. _____
4. _____
5. _____
6. _____

Role: Wife (or your next priority if you are not married)

12-Month Goal Statement: (Sample)

- I intensify our relationship by my positive words, simple gifts, increased quality time, and acts of service.

90-Day Goal Statement (Sample)

- I encourage my husband with positive words each week.

Potential Action Steps for 90-Day Goal Statement (Sample)

1. I write a note and put it in his lunch box each week.

2. I send him a positive devotion or scripture email at his work each week.

3. I thank him for one thing each night before I go to bed.

4. I refrain from saying anything negative.

5. I use only positive words to describe my husband to friends and co-workers.

Now it's your turn!

Look back at your 90-Day Goal Statement and write down simple actions that you will take in order to accomplish this goal.

Role: _____

1. _____

2. _____

3. _____

4. _____

5. _____

6. _____

Role: Mother (or your next priority if you are not a mother)

One-Year Goal Statement: (Sample)

- I teach my children biblical principles through consistent family quiet time.

   90-Day Goal Statement

   - I creatively schedule family quiet time into our busy agenda.

      Potential Action Steps for 90-Day Goal Statement

      1. I share this goal with my family this Sunday after church.

      2. I review the family calendar each week and schedule quiet time for the family.

      3. I buy a notebook for the family to list prayer requests.

      4. I buy a family devotional book for quiet time.

      5. I play worship CDs in the car for quiet time moments while driving to soccer practice.

Now it is your turn!

Look back at your 90-Day Goal Statement and write down simple actions that you will take in order to accomplish this goal.

Role: _____

1. _____

2. _____

3. _____

4. _____

5. _____

6. _____

Congratulations!

You are now ready to move forward with the changes God has inspired you to make throughout this course. This process gets easier every time you move through it. We're very excited for the commitment you have made.

We want you to succeed! We've developed a tool, *D*I*V*A*S Walk of Purpose Journal*, to help you stay focused on your daily quiet time, your accountability, and your goals. On the next two pages you'll see an example of the goal layout in the journal where you will transfer your One-Year Goals, 90-Day Goals, and the Action Steps you're committed to making each quarter. You'll have a new section for each quarter.

We've included a habit builder to help you monitor the new habits you'e incorporating into your routine. These new habits will help you become more effective and productive in creating lasting change, which will result in success!

This journal also follows the D-I-V format that you've become accustomed to through this curriculum. You have a place to journal your quiet time:

- D – Devotion to God's Word

- I – Insights/Instructions you gleaned from your daily Bible reading

- V – Prayers

We've also included an A-S page for your accountability and spiritual growth each week. This is a section that you and your accountability partner will use to guide your accountability phone call or meeting.

Your journal will create a legacy of the wonderful journey you **and God will be taking over the next year as you commit to change and improve** yourself to be the beautiful Diva God created you to be.

BRING
your *D*I*V*A*S Walk of Purpose Journal*
to class this week!

D*I*V*A*S Destiny

Role 1: Spiritual   Date: _____

One-Year Goal:

Why is this goal important to me?

90-Day Goal:

Action Steps:

1. _____
2. _____
3. _____
4. _____
5. _____
6. _____

Role 2: _____   Date: _____

One-Year Goal:

Why is this goal important to me?

90-Day Goal:

Action Steps:

1. _____
2. _____
3. _____
4. _____
5. _____
6. _____

D*I*V*A*S Destiny

Role 3: _____   Date: _____

One-Year Goal:

Why is this goal important to me?

90-Day Goal:

Action Steps:

1. _____

2. _____

3. _____

4. _____

5. _____

6. _____

Habit Builder

My habit is: I read my goals daily.

	Wk 1	Wk 2	Wk 3	Wk 4	Wk 5	Wk 6	Wk 7	Wk 8	Wk 9	Wk 10	Wk 11	Wk 12	Wk 13
Sun													
Mon													
Tue													
Wed													
Thu													
Fri													
Sat													

How to Use the Habit Builder:

It has been said that if you do something for 30 days then it becomes a habit. You have completed your goals and are starting many new habits in the upcoming month. This tool is a place where you can check off your new habit. The first habit you need to build is reading your goals everyday to stay focused and motivated. Once you have successfully mastered this habit, reading your goals will become a behavior that is part of your every day routine. Then you can add a new habit into your routine in Quarter Two.

Accountability

ACCOUNTABILITY PARTNER'S INFORMATION:

NAME: _____

PHONE: _____

       (home)   (cell)   (work)

EMAIL: _____

CONTACT DATE AND TIME: _____

Friendship Question:

Describe a past goal you have been successful in accomplishing.

Accountability Questions:

Did you complete your D*I*V*A*S devotionals this week?

What goal are you most excited about achieving?

Spiritual Growth

I will continue my spiritual growth this week by completing the following action(s):	List items your partner(s) will be focusing on for the next week. Note any prayer requests from meeting.
1. _____	1. _____
2. _____	2. _____
3. _____	3. _____

Prayer for Accountability Partner:

Oh, Father, I pray today for an accountability partner that will motivate me in achieving my dreams through her encouragement, wisdom, and Godly counsel. May we begin this journey as accountability partners and grow together as we seek your plans for us. (Proverbs 13:14-20)

WEEK 7

D∗I∗V∗A∗S Decision

Commit to the Plan

Day 1 • What's the Plan?

Sherri

As Christians, most of us know God has a plan for our lives; but sometimes we don't know what the exact plan is. We know God wants us to live for a purpose — to live out the plan He has designed for each one of us. From the Bible, we know Paul lived a purpose-driven life. According to Philippians 3:14, he said, *"I press on toward the goal to win the prize for which God has called me heavenward in Christ Jesus"* (NIV). In the Greek terminology the words used relate to running a race and finishing. So, we know Paul ran straight to the goal with purpose in every step. His only reason for living was to fulfill the plans God had for him. Paul accomplished this by staying focused on the goal, the purpose God had called him to live out.

In Proverb 20:24 we read, *"How can we understand the road we travel? It is the Lord who directs our steps."* (NLT) We all go through times when we don't know where we are going or what the plan is for our lives. I know I have. There was a season in my life when I was so unbalanced and out of focus I didn't have a clue what my purpose was. I had to re-focus on the "givens" that are a part of God's plan for every Christian. (Review the devotion on Small Steps, Week 3 Day 1.) I am working toward that intimate relationship with Him, and my life is gaining perspective. My God-given destiny is beginning to guide me.

God does have a plan and a purpose for each person. However, you must have a close intimate relationship with Him in order to discover and live out your destiny. According to Scripture, if you seek God, build a relationship with Him, and trust Him, He will guide your plans and you will know you are accomplishing your purpose in life. If you are participating in these steps, God will make your path clear.

As you continue in this week's devotions we will ask you to evaluate your commitments, activities, and priorities, to help you determine a path to guide you and encourage you as you discover your purpose and unique destiny.

Devoted

Read Psalm 20:4, James 1:5, Colossians 3:23, Philippians 4:6. Read over your goals in your journal.

Individual

What do these verses say to you about the importance of knowing and understanding God's plan for your life?

_____

_____

_____

Via – Prayer

Write a prayer asking God to help you be open to the plan He has designed for your life.

_____

_____

_____

_____

Psalm 20:4
May He give you the desire of your heart and make all your plans succeed. (NIV)

James 1:5
If any of you lacks wisdom, let him ask of God, who gives to all liberally and without reproach, and it will be given to him.

Colossians 3:23
Whatever you do, do it heartily, as to the Lord and not to men.

Philippians 4:6
Be anxious for nothing, but in everything by prayer and supplication, with thanksgiving, let your requests be made known to God.

DAY 2 • Put Your Life in the Right Order
Sherri

Has anyone ever told you you need to get your priorities in order? My grandmother used to remind me of my priorities when I was first married. Many Sundays it was just too easy to skip church. I always justified my "absence" by assuring her I could still worship God on a boat out in the middle of a lake on a beautiful 85° summer day. Or, I would tell her that after a busy work week it was the only day of the week we could sleep in without having to get up and rush around to be somewhere. Obviously, my grandmother knew where my priorities should be, and she didn't hesitate (in a loving way) to make sure I knew where my priorities should have been. I now agree with her, because I've found it to be true according to scripture that we can't live successfully without the right priorities in our lives.

According to *The Power of a Praying Woman*[16] by Stormie Omartian, our two most important priorities come directly from the Word of God. Jesus told us about them when He said, *"You shall love the Lord your God with all your heart, all your soul, and all your mind. This is the first and greatest commandment. A second is equally important: 'Love your neighbor as yourself.'"* (Matthew 22:37-39 NLT).

That's pretty clear. If you maintain these two top priorities — love God and love others — they will guide you in setting all other priorities in your life. God wants your undivided attention. He is a God of order and commitment. In I Corinthians 14:40, God's Word says, *"Let all things be done decently and in order."*

His Word tells us we need to seek His counsel on who the proper spiritual authorities should be in our lives. He wants us to be rooted and involved with other believers at church. (And yes, He also wants us to be present on beautiful summer days!) We know that if we have our lives, our priorities, our goals in order, then we will receive God's blessings. Our heart's desire should line up with God's desire for us. God will help us find the perfect balance for our life. That is clear in the following two scripture verses.

Proverb 16:3 (NIV) – *Commit to the Lord whatever you do, and your plans will succeed.*

Psalm 37:5 – *Commit your way to the Lord; trust in Him and He shall bring it to pass.*

To me, these verses mean that if we pray about our ways, our goals, our desires, our activities, and what God wants us to be committed to, we can be assured He will guide us down the right path and bless us.

Commitment is the means by which we live out our God-given intention. My personal coach (Elisa Palombi with BigLife Coaching) worked with me several years ago on commitment. She said, "As human beings we are always committed. There is no such thing as an uncommitted person; the question is what are we committed to? To find the answer, we need to only look as far as the results we have produced in our lives. What we have produced is exactly what we are committed to. The challenge of discovering our purpose is to become aware of what we are really committed to."[17]

We need to be clear about our commitments and turn them over to God in prayer. When you know what you are committed to in life, it is much easier to stay focused and balanced and live the exceptional life that God has intended for you.

So, what are you committed to? What things occupy your life? Be honest with yourself as you answer the questions on the following page. (You might as well be truthful because God already knows the following answers.)

Think about a typical week you had this month. If you use a planner or Blackberry refer to them to help you answer the questions as accurately as possible.

The exercise was very eye-opening for me.

1. How much time did you spend making money this week (your job and any other source of income)? _____

2. How much time did you spend taking care of the physical aspects of your home (cleaning, mowing, decorating, etc.)? _____

3. How much time did you spend on the day-to-day functions of keeping the household running (paying bills, laundry, cooking, planning, grocery shopping)? _____

4. How many hours did you sleep this week? _____

5. How many hours did you spend getting ready (shower, makeup)? _____

6. How many hours did you spend in the car (commuting, car pooling, errands)? _____

7. How many hours of quality time did you spend with your spouse, children? (Quality time = all members of the family engaged in an activity with a general goal of fellowship and bonding.) _____

8. How many hours did you invest in outside relationships? (Friends, extended family) _____

TOTAL HOURS _____

1. How much time did you spend with God in prayer? _____

2. How much time did you spend in His Word? _____

3. How much time did you spend in solitude getting to know Him better? _____

4. If you had an extra fifteen minutes what did you do? Watch TV? Read a magazine? Sweep the floor? Make up the bed? _____

5. So what are you committed to? What occupies most of your time?

   _____

   _____

6. What aspects of your commitments are you willing to change?

   _____

   _____

   _____

A friend once told me we should tithe our time in the same way we are supposed to tithe our money. If the average person is awake 15 hours of the day, one-tenth of that time equals 90 minutes. Break that down into three categories of 30 minutes each: 30 minutes of prayer, 30 minutes of Bible study, and 30 minutes of planning and seeking His will. How much better we would understand and know God and know that He is the Lord exercising lovingkindness, judgment, and righteousness here on this earth (Jeremiah 9:23-24) if we gave Him one-tenth of our time!

Devoted

Read Job 22:21-28. Review your goals.

Individual

Spend some time today journaling about things you are, and things you are not, committed to. You might want to refer to the devotions on Purpose (WEEK 3) and review some of the things you said you enjoyed. Review what you want said about you at your funeral (WEEK 1 DAY 5).

_____

_____

_____

_____

_____

What would you like to spend more time doing? Not doing?

_____

_____

_____

_____

_____

Via – Prayer

Write a prayer asking God to show you how to commit to His plans for you.

_____

_____

_____

_____

* * *

Day 3 • BALANCE By Design!
Donna

Joy, purpose and balance are three things that most of us desire! When we choose to live a joy-filled, purposeful, and stress-free life, it's inevitable that we will create more peace in our life.

Joy   "Joy is the infectious and uncontainable fruit of divinely inspired growth. It's a deeply entrenched, unshakable belief, the result of sustained right thinking and dwelling on the nature and character of God. Joy is an outward sign of inward faith in the promises of God. It is a way of acting, and it is evidence of spiritual maturity. Joy is not a distant destination at which you arrive; rather, it's a path you choose to travel each day. Joy is the sum and substance of emotional health. It is a state of mind that must be deliberately cultivated if you are determined to live and love and influence others as God intended."

– Tommy Newberry[18]

Purpose   Matching who you are on the inside with who you are on the outside.

Balance   Living life according to your priorities.

What do these have in common?

Simple... If you believe that you are created for a God-given purpose and you choose to live each day to fulfill your purpose, you will ultimately create more joy in your life which will make balance easier to obtain. Your thinking will be focused on the nature, character, and promises of God which will bring you emotional health, ultimate joy!

Start with purpose. We know that Scripture tells us we are created for a purpose. God designed each of us with a different purpose in mind.

You are unique! You are beautiful! You are a masterpiece! You have endless strength! You have indescribable peace! You have faith that can move mountains! The list just continues. When you align your thinking to the promises of who you are in Christ then your thoughts will shine through in your actions. This is a choice you have to make each and every day.

This leads right into joy! With a positive attitude, you can more easily overcome the stresses that can happen in your daily activities. It is typical of our human nature and our environment to focus on the negative; however, we must learn to live out Philippians 4:8 and focus only on what is lovely, pure, admirable, and praiseworthy!

When you match your thoughts up to the positive promises of God, then you will begin to defeat negative thoughts which result in negative, self-defeating actions...actions that cause you stress. When you focus on more joy and the positives in your life, you will be a light in a dark world because you will be filled with real joy!

Purpose and a positive attitude are key to helping us keep balance in our day-to-day lives. But the other important factor is to be completely aware of our priorities. What we value most should become our priorities in life. Fran and Les Hewitt's book, *The Power of Focus for Women*[19], discusses the importance of priorities, stating that if we do not live our day-to-day lives in a manner that reflects our most important values then we will not be balanced.

If family time is an important priority to you but you never spend more than one hour a weekend with your family, then you won't feel balanced. If spiritual growth is important to you yet you never pray, read the Bible, or attend a worship service then, you'll feel unbalanced or incomplete.

The key to balance is living a joy-filled life according to your priorities. As we've learned over the past several weeks, we are created to worship and serve God here on this earth and to share the Gospel with a lost world. This is priority one. So, if you agree that the key to balance is living life according to your priorities, then for you balance means spending time with God each day. Focusing on your spouse is priority number two, followed by focusing on your children. By having a written set of goals that fall in line with your priorities and commitments, you can stay focused on what is important to you — which helps reduce stress and create more peace and balance in your life.

What do you value? What are your priorities? Circle your top five from the list below:

Family Ties	A Quality Marriage	Education
Lasting Health	Financial Peace	Honesty
Integrity	Quiet Time	Success
Reputation	Spiritual Growth	Appearance
Serving Others	Learning New Things	Friends
Positive Attitude	Balanced Schedule	Family Traditions

Ephesians 5:15-17 (NIV) tell us: *Be very careful, then, how you live – not as unwise but as wise, making the most of every opportunity, because the days are evil. Therefore do not be foolish, but understand what the Lord's will is.* God's Word clearly states that we are to know His will and live a life of purpose by making every opportunity count! We can only do this when we

choose to keep God at the center of our life. When He is the center of our priorities, we can be certain our priorities will fall into place.

If you want to have balance in your life, make sure your everyday life incorporates your top five priorities.

List five ways you are incorporating your priorities into your day-to-day routine.

1. _____
2. _____
3. _____
4. _____
5. _____

In Summary:

Joy comes from sustained right thinking and faith in God's hierarchy of priorities, even though it isn't the easy or the worldly standards that surround us. Real joy, authentic joy, joy you experience regardless of your circumstances, truly comes from choosing God as your number one priority.

Purpose is living according to the way God designed you — again, living according to God's priorities and doing the things He has called you to do. If you aren't living with God's purpose you won't experience real joy!

Balance comes from choosing to spend time and energy on God's hierarchy of priorities. If you make this choice as a part of your daily routine, you can be guaranteed a new sense of balance in your life! That doesn't mean you won't have crazy, hectic days; but on these days you will still experience authentic joy and purpose!

Your goals will help you stay focused on God's purpose and plan in your life. They will be a road map to help you reach your daily destination of authentic joy!

Devoted

Read Proverb 19:21 and Ephesians 1:11. Review your goals.

Individual

When you believe you are living a life of purpose according to your God-given skills, talents and abilities, your life will be more balanced. What is God saying to you today about maintaining your priorities in life in order to give you balance?

Proverb 19:21
You can make many plans, but the LORD's purpose will prevail. (NLT)

Ephesians 1:11
Furthermore, because of Christ, we have received an inheritance from God, for he chose us from the beginning, and all things happen just as he decided long ago. (NLT)

_____

_____

_____

_____

_____

_____

Via - Prayer

Write a prayer asking God to keep you focused on your values so you maintain balance.

_____

_____

_____

_____

_____

_____

_____

_____

DAY 4 • Choose Who You Want to Become
Sherri

We have talked about what we are committed to and what we begin to see when our priorities fall into place. As Christian women, we have no greater responsibility than to determine what we were put here on earth to accomplish. Each of us has a God-given purpose and mission. What if we all had our purposes and missions written down on a piece of paper? Would that help us stay more focused on our calling in life?

I have worked on my Life Purpose Statement and goals for several years, but it is always a work in progress. As I grow in Christ, my goals and my Life Purpose Statements continue to change and grow. I love to read. I am always looking for self-growth books to help me grow personally and spiritually. (Doesn't that sound better than self-help?) Look at two verses from the best self-help book ever written.

John 17:18 (MSG): *"In the same way that you gave me a mission in the world, I give them a mission in the world."*

Acts 20:24: *"None of these things move me; nor do I count my life dear to myself, so that I may finish my race with joy, and the ministry which I received from the Lord Jesus, to testify to the gospel of the grace of God."*

In his book *Success Is Not An Accident* Tommy Newberry defined a Life Purpose Statement in the following way:

> It is a written articulation of exactly what type of person you ultimately want to become. It expresses your unique purpose for living. Your Life Purpose Statement encourages you to change in a deliberate, preconceived direction. The process of constructing a Life Purpose Statement forces you to seriously think through the vital areas of your life. Creating a Life Purpose Statement requires reflection, introspection, and a considerable quantity of mental effort. [20]

It's not as hard as it sounds. It just takes a little bit of your time and a little bit of your commitment. Actually, you've already done most of the hard work. You've thought about and worked through vital areas of your life; you've completed some introspective assessments; and you've already invested a lot of mental effort and prayer. Compiling it and writing it down on paper is all you have left to do. Simply write on paper what you want your legacy to be (the person you want to be, the person that you are created to be, the person God expects you to be). The benefit of having a written Life Purpose Statement is that it validates your responsibility and commitment to living a life dedicated to God's purpose. The rest of your life should revolve around Your Life Purpose Statement. Your mission should be what you want others to see in you.

Have fun with it! What vision do you see of yourself? What is your ultimate purpose in life? Your Life Purpose Statement doesn't have to be long. It's just a broad synopsis of what's important in your life. You should write it in present tense as if it has already happened and you are already that person.

For example, my Life Purpose Statement used to be this (don't forget, it's ever-changing!):

> I am an ultra-positive person who shares my enthusiasm for life with others. I exemplify my spiritual beliefs through words and actions. I find it easy to maintain a healthy balance between home and work. I make a difference in other people's lives because my inspiration helps others strive for a new level of energy and passion in their lives. I am physically fit because I have chosen a lifestyle of balanced food choices and consistent exercise. I am a joy to be around!

Now, I've simplified it: I gain inspiration by encouraging, motivating, and equipping others to succeed.

Other examples might be more simple or more complex; it's a personal statement. The following are some other examples.

Life Purpose Statement by a stay-at-home mom:

I have a genuine godly impact on the people who are a part of my life through my unconditional love, my passion to grow spiritually, and my day-to-day example.

Life Purpose Statement by a business owner:

Through my passion for life I attract motivated individuals, and through my relationships I create an environment for positive change.

Life Purpose Statement by a corporate CEO:

To live my life so I help my husband, my children, and myself get to heaven with many crowns to lay at Jesus' feet.

Now, I'll be the first to admit — and I'm sure my husband will agree — there are days I don't live up to my Life Purpose Statement (but not too often, I hope!).

It will be the same for you. However, when you have a day, week, or even a month that doesn't go as you've planned, you can always read back over your Life Purpose Statement. It will help you get back on track and remind you of the wonderful person God created you to be. It will remind you to persevere, to take up your cross, and continue to run the race. It will give you clarity and re-direction.

Jot down a list of bulleted ideas of what you want to include in your Life Purpose Statement. Think about what impact you want to make on others. What do you want to be known for? What is your main purpose in life?

_____

_____

_____

_____

Matthew 28:18-20

Jesus came to them and said, "All authority in heaven and on earth has been given to me. Therefore go and make disciples of all nations, baptizing them in the name of the Father and of the Son and of the Holy Spirit, and teaching them to obey everything I have commanded you. And surely I am with you always, to the very end of the age. (NIV)

Joshua 1:8

Do not let this Book of the Law depart from your mouth; meditate on it day and night, so that you may be careful to do everything written in it. Then you will be prosperous and successful. (NIV)

Devoted

Read Matthew 28:18-20, Joshua 1:8. Review your goals.

Individual

In Mathew 28:18-20 (known as the Great Commission), God commands us to live according to his commandment. In Joshua, we are commanded to meditate on God's Word and apply it to our life so we can be successful and prosperous. How will your Life Purpose Statement accomplish these principles?

_____

_____

_____

_____

_____

_____

Via - Prayer

Write a prayer asking God to give you wisdom and insights regarding what He wants your mission in life to be.

_____

_____

_____

_____

_____

_____

_____

_____

DAY 5 • My Life Purpose Statement
Sherri

Spend some time today working on your Life Purpose Statement. Go back through your devotions focusing on the self assessments, the personal questions regarding how you want to change, what you want to be known for at your funeral, what you want to be committed to, your most important roles and the bulleted items you jotted down in yesterday's devotion. Review your life map and imagine where you want it to go in the future. What passions or patterns do you see in your past that you want to be in your future?

Your Life Purpose Statement should direct your life. Proverb 4:26 tells us, *"Mark out a straight path for your feet; then stick to the path and stay safe"* (NLT). If your Life Purpose Statement keeps you moving in the right direction, won't that make your feel successful? What a great feeling to know that you're living life with a purpose — the life God intended for you! When you live out your God-focused Life Purpose Statement, you'll make a difference in others' lives, too!

Think about King David. Despite the fact that he ran into some trouble and lost site of his priorities for a while, he did dedicate his life to serving God. He made serving God his purpose in life. Acts 13:36 tells us that *David had served God's purpose in his own generation* (NIV). Can't you imagine David's Life Purpose Statement simply reading: I am a man after God's own heart. I will obediently serve God so my ways are not only pleasing to Him but a great example to others.

After you have reviewed this information, stop and pray for God to give you the wisdom and discernment you need to put your mission statement, your purpose, your unique ministry into words. Don't hesitate. Just start writing. Remember to be creative. Make it fun! Make it you!

My Life Purpose Statement

_____

_____

_____

_____

_____

_____

Devoted

Read John 17:18, Acts 20:24, 2 Corinthians 6:4-10. These scriptures reflect possible Life Purpose Statements from Jesus and from Paul. Read your goals.

Individual

What have you concluded is your main mission in life? What examples did you discover from Paul's words?

_____

_____

_____

_____

Via - Prayer

Write a prayer of thanks to God for giving you wisdom and insight in writing your Life Purpose Statement, for giving you a purpose in life and for making you the beautiful D*I*V*A that you are!

_____

_____

_____

_____

John 17:18

In the same way that you gave me a mission in the world, I give them a mission in the world. (MSG)

Acts 20:24

The most important thing is that I complete my mission, the work that the Lord Jesus gave me. (NCV)

2 Corinthians 6:4-10

In everything we do we try to show that we are true ministers of God. We patiently endure troubles and hardships and calamities of every kind. We have been beaten, been put in jail, faced angry mobs, worked to exhaustion, endured sleepless nights, and gone without food. We have proved ourselves by our purity, our understanding, our patience, our kindness, our sincere love, and the power of the Holy Spirit. We have faithfully preached the truth. Gods power has been working in us....We serve God whether people honor us or despise us, whether they slander us or praise us. We are honest... (NLT)

Accountability

ACCOUNTABILITY PARTNER'S INFORMATION:

NAME: _____

PHONE: _____
            (home)   (cell)   (work)

EMAIL: _____

CONTACT DATE AND TIME: _____

Friendship Question:

What are you most excited about this week that relates to your purpose in life?

Accountability Questions:

Did you complete your D*I*V*A*S devotionals this week?

What is your Life Purpose statement?

Did you read your goals each day?

Spiritual Growth

I will continue my spiritual growth this week by completing the following action(s):	List items your partner(s) will be focusing on for the next week. Note any prayer requests from meeting.
1. _____	1. _____
2. _____	2. _____
3. _____	3. _____

Prayer for Accountability Partner:

Dear Father, help me find a sister in Christ that will support me in completing the mission You have for my life. May we encourage each other in living a life based on Your priorities. (Acts 20:24)

WEEK 8

D*I*V*A*S DESTINY
EQUIPPED FOR HIS WORK

DAY 1 • Accountability Time

Sherri

Last week you focused on your plan and determined what you are committed to. You've developed a personal Life Purpose Statement that reflects your commitment to God's plan in your life. You've also developed a plan to help you become all God wants you to be in the three most important roles in your life. Now, what? Once these plans are in place according to God's will in your life, where do you go from here?

You've completed this process, now it is time for you to move forward with God's plan in your life. Ephesians 2:10 tells us *we are God's workmanship, created in Christ Jesus to do good works, which God prepared in advance for us to do* (NIV). If He prepared you to do His work, that's what He wants you to be doing. In order to successfully move toward these good works, it's important to surround yourself with positive individuals who will help you stay on track and continually encourage you.

Proverb 11:14 says *where there is no counsel, the people fall; but in the multitude of counselors there is safety.* Who belongs in your "council?" It's time to start looking for the right people who can help you stay accountable to the call God has placed on your life, your ministry, your unique purpose.

In looking for someone to talk with about your plan and purpose, look for someone who is loyal, someone who shares your vision, someone who you know has faith and integrity. Yes, you're finally ready to begin the search for your own individual accountability partner! This is someone you have already been praying for throughout this study.

To be accountable literally means to stand up — to be counted for. Acountability is protection against our natural human tendency towards self-deception. True accountability provides a great source of information on how we can improve our lives. None of us has the insight or strength to always make the right choices. Accountability helps, guides, and encourages you to live according to God's Word, even in times of temptation.[21]

In Week 1, we talked about the many advantages of an accountability partner. Everyone needs the love, support, and help of others. Have you found your accountability partner? If not, have you been thinking of anyone who could be a great accountability partner for you? Has God brought a specific person's name to you over the past few weeks? What type of accountability do you feel would work best for you? (Refer to The Jewels of Accountability in Week 1.) If this person is still not evident in your life, keep praying for God to reveal her to you. Most importantly, pray for God's will in this relationship, even if the person God is laying on your heart doesn't "fit" or make sense to you right now. Trust in God, and be obedient to Him. He knows what is best for you.

As you begin using the *D*I*V*A*S Walk of Purpose Journal* and scheduling weekly accountability meetings to reach your D*I*V*A*S Destiny, use the following Do's and Don'ts, the Individual Preparation Guidelines and the Accountability Timeline as a guide. Review these with your partner and make sure both of you are in agreement on the format and structure of your meetings.

Where there is no counsel, the people fall;
but in the multitude of counselors there is safety. Proverb 11:14

Accountability Do's

- Maximize your time by following the suggested timeline of 15 minutes per person.

- Keep Accountability appointments brief and business like.

- Start and stop appointments on time.

- Keep conversations focused on your goals and strategic actions.

- **Add** a Sapphire or Amethyst Accountability relationship after you have mastered either a Ruby or Diamond relationship.

- Take responsibility for your actions.

- Commit to the covenant traits of honesty, commitment, confidentiality, and transparency for effective accountability.

- Pre-set all appointments.

- Ask penetrating questions to help each other grow.

- Challenge each other in areas of growth.

- Be prepared for your meeting. Review your successes, struggles and desired actions for change prior to meeting. Remember the *I* in D*I*V*A*S is for *Individual.*

- Do offer weekly support through encouraging emails, phone calls, and cards.

Accountability Don'ts

- Don't view Accountability meetings and calls as social visits. Schedule social activities at different times or as an **addition** to your accountability appointment.

- Don't utilize Accountability meetings for in-depth Bible study. Bible studies are encouraged as a great way to deepen relationships and to reach personal goals but they should be viewed as a separate part of the spiritual growth process.

- Don't make excuses for you actions.

- Don't try to schedule appointments on a week-to-week basis.

- Don't be late for you appointed accountability meeting.

- Don't forget to bring your *D*I*V*A*S Walk of Purpose Journal* to each meeting.

In *D*I*V*A*S* the "I" Is for Individual

She is a woman willing to take full responsibility for her choices, regardless of her past or her current circumstances. She is surrendering everything for the glory of God, allowing HIM to heal and use her weakness and brokenness for the ministry He has set before her.

The following is a list of items you are responsible for prior to your Accountability Appointment. We have also included a breakdown of the suggested 15-minute timeline for you to follow. This will allow for each person to have an equal opportunity in the accountability process.

Individual Accountability Preparation

- Take time each week prior to the scheduled appointment to review the past week by completing the AS page in the *Walk of Purpose Journal* and rating your progress.

- Be prepared to share a couple of successes from the past week.

- Write the three action items you want to accomplish for the upcoming week. Be realistic with your expectations of yourself. Remember that small steps will move you toward accomplishing your 90-Day Goal. However, by committing to this exercise, you should expect to be challenged by your partner(s).

- If, due to scheduling, travel, vacation, etc. you cannot make the appointment on a particular scheduled date, you are responsible for making sure the meeting is rescheduled.

Accountability Timeline (15 minutes per person)

- Spend five minutes to review the personal accountability questions for this quarter. (You will learn about accountability questions in Day 2.)

- Spend five minutes sharing your victories and successes from this past week.

- Spend five minutes sharing the action steps for improvement that you will put into place for the upcoming week. This is where your partner(s) will be able to make suggestions for further improvement.

Devoted

Read the Ecclesiastes verses in the sidebar and underline the many advantages you will find in an accountability relationship.

Individual

List names of any people you have thought about asking to be your accountability partner and why you think they would be a good partner for you. Write down which Jewels of Accountability you feel would best fit your needs right now.

_____

_____

_____

Via – Prayer

Write a prayer asking God to continue to guide you with wisdom in finding your accountability partner. If you have already found your partner, write a prayer asking God to bless your new accountability relationship.

_____

_____

_____

_____

Ecclesiastes 4:9-12

Two are better than one, because they have a good reward for their labor. For if they fall, one will lift up his companion. But woe to him who is alone when he falls, for he has no one to help him up. Again, if two lie down together, they will keep warm; but how can one be warm alone? Though one may be overpowered by another, two can withstand him. And a threefold cord is not quickly broken.

The "A" in D•I•V•A•S Is for ACCOUNTABLE

She is a woman willing to be accountable to God's Word and willing to encourage fellow sisters in Christ to do the same. She is willing to search out the truth in God's Word and apply it to every facet of her life, and share God's truth in love with her fellow D•I•V•A•S.

DAY 2
Now We Know What Account-a-what-a Is
Sherri

I am thinking back to the devotion titled Account-a-what-a? I'll bet when we first started this journey together you were also thinking account-a-what-a?! After all, we don't always like being accountable to any account-a-who-a-ability partner. It's scary. It means we have to "report in" to someone each week. If we didn't meet our goals for the week, we feel the need to give our accountability partner excuses of why we didn't do the things we agreed we would do. But we must remember, we are all a work in progress, and as humans we will never be perfect.

I thought about this concept as I wrote this. When I had biopsies on two skin spots, one on each leg, I met with the doctor, who confirmed they were sun cancer. He called it "superficial" cancer, which means it is under the top layer of the skin and needs to be cut out to make sure we get it all. He said he could burn it off, which would leave less of a scar; but he recommended cutting it out to be sure we didn't leave any of the cancer. This isn't the first time this doctor has removed sunspots for me.

I love being in the sun. I found myself wanting to argue with the doctor and state my case for why I need to have a tan in the summer. I wanted to know if I had to completely give up this pleasure I love. I asked him if, when I went on a tropical vacation, I had to sit under a palm tree and read my book. He sincerely and calmly said, "Of course not. You can sit out in the sun as long as you have SPF 60 tanning lotion on!"

"SPF 60!" I shrieked. "I thought 45 SPF was the highest you could get. What's the point?" He reminded me that the "point" was to remain healthy, and guard my skin against further sun damage and more cancerous spots. He reminded me that I am now primed for skin cancer every time I go out in the sun. He also reminded me that these two particular spots were worse than the ones previously removed from my arms and chest area.

I sat there in disbelief while he tried to counsel me and tell me that I could revert to spray-on tans and tanning lotions from a bottle. At this particular moment I wasn't as concerned about the actual "skin spots" as I was about how deathly white I would look in the summertime. It was then I realized how silly I was being. This was a wake-up call that I needed to give up something in my life that was not good for me in order to be healthier and to avoid really bad cancer. Immediately, I knew I needed someone to make me put SPF 60 on and someone to remind me of the reason I need to use sunscreen — I needed accountability.

I went with a girlfriend to a tropical beach that summer. Even before we left I was already envisioning days of just basking in the sun while reading a book. I told her about my appointment and that I needed her to remind me on vacation to keep the 60 SPF on. (I actually called it the blasted 60 SPF — see, I was still in denial!) I needed to share that with her so she could help me be accountable, because I know I am weak in this area. Even in the past, when I've had other spots removed, I continued to sun-bake with very low SPF lotions.

Reaching goals in your life is much easier when you have someone to support you. An accountability partner can help you see things in a different perspective and can encourage you when you feel down or when you didn't accomplish as much as you wanted to. Have you found your accountability partner yet? I guarantee that when you have the right person in place, she will become more than an accountability partner to you. She will become a dear and trusted friend that you will feel very blessed to have!

Devoted

Read through your goals and give yourself a check on the habit builder. Don't lose faith. God has an accountability partner in mind for you. Continue to persevere through dedicated prayer. Read Hebrews 10:35-36.

Hebrews 10:35-36
Do not throw away your confidence; it will be richly rewarded. You need to persevere so that when you have done the will of God, you will receive what he has promised. (NIV)

Individual

Throughout the last seven weeks you have been participating in accountability phone calls. We have provided you with simple weekly Accountability questions to review with your partner to ask each other. You now have your own written goals and action steps to help you reach your D*I*V*A*S Destiny! As you have learned, if you don't have someone to support, encourage, and challenge you with your goals it will be easy for you to slip, forget, or simply stop moving forward.

Look back over your goals and develop three questions your accountability partner will ask you each week at your meeting. (One question related to each of your goals). This question should be a simple yes or no type question that reflects whether or not you are taking the small steps you have committed to in your quarterly action plan.

The Three Questions I Want My Accountability Partner To Ask Me:

1. _____

   _____

2. _____

   _____

3. _____

   _____

Via - Prayer

As you pray today, ask God to clarify who you should be contacting for your accountability partner. Once you receive confirmation, pick up the phone and call her. Yes, pick up that phone today and make a positive step toward moving your life in an awesome direction! (Have you called her yet?)

_____

_____

_____

_____

If you do have a partner, pray for her and the weekly discussions you will have together. Pray both of you will exhibit the attributes of an accountable person. Pray you will accept the truth and encouragement she gives you even if it's not what you want to hear. Pray for your accountability relationship to turn into a great friendship that will help you move in the direction that God has designed for you. Pray you both will always remain D*I*V*A*S.

You are going to love account-a-what-a! It's really awesome!

_____

_____

_____

_____

_____

_____

_____

_____

DAY 3 • Enjoy the Process
Sherri

"Enjoy the Process" may not sound like an exciting title for today's devotion but let me share with you what that means to me. I am a person who likes structure and organization. I like things to be in order. My desk and my house have to be tidy 99.9% of the time for my personal sanity. Some may call this Type A. I just call it Me. It's been me for as long as I can remember.

Now I'm going through a "process" of looking for symptoms and triggers that have made me this way. My downfall is that I have such a strong need for organization that I have sometimes been known to forsake my family, my need for sleep, or some fun activity in order to stay up late and "complete" the tasks on my desk or to finish a home project I've been working on. I have a need for "completion." It makes me feel more "organized" when I have these things checked off my list — Finished, Completed — and ready to move on to the next project. Another problem with my downfall is that God does not work according to my need for organization and completion. He likes to do things His way!

I'm sure it has crossed your mind by this point, that perhaps I am a bit of a control freak, too! It's true — I do like to control my environment the best I can. My personal coach has talked with me about this "issue" more than once. Again, I call it Me; but she calls it Something We Are Going to Work On! I like Me just the way I am. However, I know that in order to experience personal and spiritual growth I must surrender my need for control.

She has explained the problem with my downfalls by comparing life to a river. If I picture myself as the river, I am going through a process of crashing on the rocks, going through ups and downs, and around bends and curves until I eventually get to the sea. She reminds me that we can't forget the law of natural gravity. If we try to go against gravity and do things that don't flow with the natural flow of the river, then we will create chaos in our lives. Once that river flows into the sea, the journey is over, and if we are not careful, we will find ourselves left saying, "Now what? What was the point?"

For me personally, she is reminding me I need to learn to enjoy the "process" of whatever I am working on or experiencing. I don't have to try and force the river into the sea (complete the project as rapidly as possible). I should focus on enjoying the "flow" of the experience and the different turns it will take. Yes, there are times when the project will hit a huge rock or boulder. It will be shattered in all directions. It might take a turn I wasn't prepared for or in control of. It might also hit some rocky rapids with lots of altering white water. It might take a class five drop and sink to the bottom of the river. Or, it might even get stuck in those circular currents you can't get out of. But that is all part of the process I need to accept.

If you think about it — it's no different than the life God has in store for each of us. He is taking us through a process in our lives. His Word tells us He is continually refining us to bring us to a true representation of His glory here on earth. His job is to make us more Christ-like through each process. Every process we go through works toward this goal.

You are in a process right now with the life changes (goals) you have been working on. You are also beginning to fine tune your relationship with your accountability partner. Perhaps you are one who is continuing to pray that God will lead you to the right accountability partner.

We need to remind ourselves that the river will flow rapidly and in the right direction much of the time, but there will be "crashes against the rocks" from time to time, too. We can't fight the law of natural gravity. In other words, life happens. We just have to maintain our faith through prayer and continue on around the next curve in the river. Eventually things will smooth out. God's grace will be sufficient through these rough waters. The important thing is to enjoy the process and not give up on it just because the water gets a little rough.

In Isaiah 66:12 the Lord says, *"I will extend peace to her like a river, and the wealth of nations like a flooding stream; you will nurse and be carried on her arm and dandled on her knees."* (NIV)

You can't always choose how you want your "river in life to flow." However, you can choose to accept the peace God has promised, "enjoy the process," and be content with where you are at the moment. After all, that is exactly where God wants you to be. It is a choice.

For me, I am choosing not to stress when I don't complete a project according to my personal time frame. I am choosing to enjoy obstacles I face by surrendering them to God and seeking His glory in the challenges.

You can be content and enjoy whatever the process when you are daily living in the presence of God. Will you make that choice, too?

Enjoy where you are right now in your life. Enjoy working on the goals you have established during the last seven weeks. Choose to enjoy the conversation you will have each week with your accountability partner. Choose to get back on track with your goals when you have a week that you don't look at them at all. You can choose to enjoy your own process! Take time this week to just simply enjoy whatever you are doing.

Devoted

Read the following verses on contentment. Focus on finding contentment in your current circumstances. Find the joy and focus on the positive. Today also spend some time reflecting on the contentment and joy you will discover as you complete your goals over the course of the next year!

Read Ecclesiastes 3:11-12, Hebrews 13:5-6, Job 36:11, and 1 Timothy 6:6. Write Philippians 4:11-13 on the lines below.

_____

_____

_____

_____

Ecclesiastes 3:11-12
He has made everything beautiful in its time... I know that nothing is better for them than to rejoice, and to do good in their lives.

Hebrews 13:5-6
Let your conduct be without covetousness; be content with such things as you have. For He Himself has said, " I will never leave you nor forsake you." So we may boldly say: "The LORD is my helper; I will not fear. What can man do to me?"

Job 36:11
If they obey and serve Him, They shall spend their days in prosperity, And their years in pleasures.

1 Timothy 6:6
Now godliness with contentment is great gain.

Individual

Take a few minutes to visualize yourself sitting on the bank of a river, the sun beaming down on you while you listen to the comforting sounds of the water rushing over the rocks, the birds chirping, the wind rustling in the trees. Now, close your eyes and think about the projects, activities, trials, and challenges you are facing this week and remember you can do all things with God's help.

What has God revealed to you regarding your circumstances right now?

_____

_____

_____

_____

_____

_____

Via – Prayer

Write a prayer and ask God to give you the joy of contentment and peace throughout this "process."

_____

_____

_____

_____

_____

_____

_____

_____

Day 4 • Pulse Check
Sherri

Time for a pulse check! Think back to Week 1 when we first began the process of talking about goals and accountability. Was your heart racing? Were you wondering what you had gotten yourself into? Well, congratulations!!

- **You** still have a pulse after eight weeks of stepping out of your comfort zone!

- **You** are an amazing woman who has just reached a new milestone in your life!

- **You** have done it!

- **You** are responsible for the time you have spent focusing on God's direction for your life.

- **You** have chosen to focus on the goals in your life that you know God wants you to be working on!

- **You** have chosen to seek out an accountability partner who can help you move forward with your own personal journey.

YOU ARE AWESOME!

So, how does your pulse feel now? Is it beating calmly and with less anxiety than you possibly had eight weeks ago? It should be a normal but excited heartbeat now, because you have a clear sense of direction in which you are going.

This is our last week of devotions together. We're proud of your personal accomplishments and the changes you're making in your life! You should be proud of yourself, too!

Devoted

Review your goals today! Don't forget to put a check on the habit builder in the *D*I*V*A*S Walk of Purpose Journal*. Read Philippians 4:6-7.

Individual

Philippians 4:6-7
Be anxious for nothing, but in everything by prayer and supplication, with thanksgiving, let your requests be made known to God; and the peace of God, which surpasses all understanding, will guard your hearts and minds through Christ Jesus.

In the verses you just read, the words *peace* and *heart* stand out to us. Do you have peace in your heart? If so you can be assured you are moving in the right direction to accomplish your D*I*V*A*S Destiny. You have prayed for wisdom and guidance throughout this study. We hope you feel a true peace about which direction God is leading you. It's okay if the big picture seems cloudy or vague. You have established steps to continue in your spiritual walk and if you are true to these steps through accountability and prayer, then your predetermined destiny is awaiting you. In God's time, it will become fully clear to you. Remember our story: We didn't even know each other, nor did we ever imagine this curriculum would develop from that first step. The first step: Pray for an accountability person in your life. The second step: Obey God and follow His direction.

As this journey comes to an end, we hope you have discovered a true peace that surpasses all understanding, a clear understanding of your unique ministry in God's kingdom, and a deeper understanding and desire for accountability in your life. Finally, we hope you now have deeper relationships with other sisters in Christ.

What is your biggest "peace" in completing this curriculum and beginning to add some accountability in your life?

_____

_____

_____

_____

Via – Prayer

You can continue to enjoy the journey by working toward the habit of praying each day, taking a couple of minutes to review your goals, and track your success and struggles in your journal, and being committed to your accountability partner once a week. You've done the work. Now, all you need to do is reap the benefits God promises you will receive from this process! Write a prayer asking God to help you stay on track by reviewing your goals each day and focusing on the changes He has led you to pursue.

_____

_____

_____

_____

_____

_____

* * *

DAY 5 • Dedicated Time
Sherri

This part of the D*I*V*A*S study is over. Now you are equipped with tools to help you create joy, balance, and accountability in your life! You have your Life Purpose Statement written down. You have established some action steps and goals to help you become all God created you to be. You should be in the process of finding and establishing accountability in your life.

Now you have to put a new habit into place. In order to stay focused and accomplish your goals, you need to review them often. You should review your D*I*V*A*S Destiny goals in your *D*I*V*A*S Walk of Purpose Journal* every day. Make it a consistent habit.

Sometimes we just get lazy and don't want to think about one more thing in our day. However, we need to focus on being purposeful about the time we spend with God each day for prayer, quiet time, and reviewing our D*I*V*A*S Destiny. We must have a set place and time to meet with God — study His Word (D), reflect (I), pray (V), and review your action steps.

Sometimes your "busy" schedule keeps you from praying or spending quality quiet time with your Father — the Holy One who, in fact, can calm your hectic life if you just choose to spend quality time with Him. You need to schedule a daily date with God. Things that don't get scheduled don't get done. God is important, so you should desire to block out a time slot in your schecule for Him. After all, you owe Him one-tenth of your time, right? Your prayer and quiet time is a personal choice. It should be a normal part of your day...as normal as making that first pot of coffee or making the bed in the morning. Make it work for you!

Today, spend some time with God in prayer and then take a few minutes to read over your goals. It's important to remember there will be days you won't be able to review your goals for "whatever" reasons. It's ok. Don't get discouraged; just re-focus your commitment to God and to yourself. Just having your goals written and reviewing them a few times a week is more progress than you've been accustomed to! Keep up the good work!

Devoted

Read the following verse out of Proverbs and circle the action words you should take each day.

Proverbs 4:25-27

> Let your eyes look straight ahead, fix your gaze directly before you. Make level paths for your feet and take only ways that are firm. Do not swerve to the right or the left; keep your foot from evil (NIV).

Individual

If you keep your focus on God, He will direct your steps and guide your accomplishments. What are you most excited about accomplishing this year? Why?

_____

_____

_____

_____

Via - Prayer

Pray and thank God today for the goals you've set for yourself. Thank Him in advance for the success He is going to give you this year.

_____

_____

_____

_____

Dear Sister,

We hope the tools we have shown you through D*I*V*A*S of the Divine become part of your daily walk with God. We hope you have a deeper understanding of your purpose here on earth. Our continued prayer is for you to be a truly devoted individual who is always making positive change in your life through prayer, accountability and spiritual growth.

Thank you for allowing us to be part of your journey toward your D*I*V*A*S Destiny. May God richly bless you!

In His Love,
Donna and Sherri

End Notes

1. Tommy Newberry, *Success Is Not An Accident*, (Decatur, GA: Looking Glass Books, 1999) © Tommy Newberry.

2. Janet Thompson, *Woman to Woman Mentoring*, (Nashville, TN: LifeWay Press, 2000) © Janet Thompson, p. 79.

3. Rick Warren, *The Purpose of Christmas* (New York, NY: Howard Books, a division of Simon & Schuster, Inc., 2008), © Rick Warren, p 30.

4. Cheri Fuller, *A Busy Woman's Guide to Prayer*, (Brentwood, TN: Integrity Publishers, 2005), Cheri Fuller, p. 135.

5. Cheri Fuller, *A Busy Woman's Guide to Prayer*, (Brentwood, TN: Integrity Publishers, 2005), Cheri Fuller, pp. 11-12.

6. Gail MacDonald, "High Call, High Privilege" from *Joy for the Journey* (Wheaton, IL: Tyndale, 1984)

7. Stormie Omartian, *The Power of a Praying Woman*, (Eugene, OR: Harvest House Publishers, 2002) © Stormie Omartian, p. 134

8. David Francis, *Spiritual Gifts, A Practical Guide to How God Works Through You*, (Nashville, TN: LifeWay Press, © 2003)

9. Vine, W. E. "Forgive, Forgave, Forgiveness," *Vine's Expository Dictionary of New Testament Words*. Blue Letter Bible. 1940. 1 Apr 2007. 17 Mar 2010.

10. Joanna Weaver, *Having a Mary Spirit*, (Colorado Springs, CO: WaterBrook Press 2006) © Joanna Weaver, p. 51

11. Tommy Newberry, *Success Is Not An Accident*, (Decatur, GA: Looking Glass Books, 1999) © Tommy Newberry.

12. Tommy Newberry, *Success Is Not An Accident*, (Decatur, GA: Looking Glass Books, 1999) © Tommy Newberry.

13. Tommy Newberry, *Success Is Not An Accident*, (Decatur, GA: Looking Glass Books, 1999) © Tommy Newberry.

14. Beth Moore, *Believing God*, (Nashville, TN: Life Way Press, 2002) © Beth Moore.

15. Dr. Greg Frizzell, *How to Develop a Powerful Prayer Life*, (Memphis, TN: Master Design in cooperation with Master Design Ministries, 1999)

16. Stormie Omartian, *The Power of a Praying Woman*, (Eugene, OR: Harvest House Publishers, 2002) © Stormie Omartian, p. 96.

17. Elisa Palmombi, BigLife Executive Coaching and Consulting, www.biglifegroup.com

18. Tommy Newberry, *The 4:8 Principle*, (Carol Stream, IL: Tyndale House Publishers, Inc., 2007) © Tommy Newbery, p.6

19. Fran & Les Hewitt, *The Power of Focus for Women*, (Deerfield Beach, Florida: Health Communications, Inc. © 2003)

20. Tommy Newberry, *Success Is Not An Accident*, (Decatur, GA: Looking Glass Books, 1999) © Tommy Newberry.

21. Tommy Newberry, *Success In Not An Accident*, Secrets of the 1% Club, (U.S.: The 1% Club, Inc. 2006), © Tommy Newbery p. 84

About the Authors

Donna McCrary and Sherri Holbert are Professional Life Coaches certified through the American Association of Christian Counselors. Their friendship began as mere acquaintances in the same small group, where God led Sherri to ask Donna to be her spiritual accountability partner. In the years since, this dynamic team has encouraged, supported and inspired each other to live out God's plan for their lives.

Now, they have combined their education, experience and passion to create an equally dynamic eight-week life-coaching curriculum full of innovative and tangible action plans designed to ensure others have the same opportunity for growth and success in all areas of life. In fact, *D*I*V*A*S of the Divine* includes the same tools Donna and Sherri use to guide their own walks, and was the inspiration for development of their Walk of Purpose Ministry (www.walkofpurpose.com).

Donna McCrary

From high top basketball shoes to high heels, each step of Donna's life has equipped her for a Life Coaching career. She is a challenging facilitator whose "tell it like it is" approach always incorporates a "call to action" from her participants.

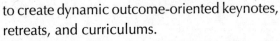

Donna draws from her background as a Recreational Therapist to create dynamic outcome-oriented keynotes, retreats, and curriculums.

Her greatest passion and deepest joy is to coach women in realizing God's plan for their lives and discovering for themselves the source of genuine joy.

Donna is a wife, mother of two, and a beloved friend. Her hobbies include hiking, vacationing at the beach, and trying projects from popular HGTV home improvement shows... much to her husband's dismay!

Sherri Holbert

Sherri has invested many years with companies such as Biltmore Estate, Chick-fil-A, and Chimney Rock Park, developing new and creative programs to propel these corporations to higher levels of success.

She is founder and CEO of Power-Up! a coaching company whose mission is to take individuals and corporations to the next level of success.

Sherri works as a coach, facilitator, and speaker for a variety of clients ranging from corporate executives to stay-at-home moms. Her passion is unlocking the untapped potential within others to help them gain fresh perspectives, develop clear vision, and establish steps that will make their dreams a reality.

Sherri, a wife, aunt, and friend to many, has a self-proclaimed addiction to shoes, purses and Starbuck's Coffee. One of her life goals is to be a contestant on her favorite TV reality show – Survivor!

WE WANT TO KNOW WHAT YOU THINK ABOUT THIS STUDY!

Please share your comments about this study by posting your review on our website. From the menu bar at the top of the Hensley Publishing home page, select Bible Studies. On the Bible Studies page, scroll down until you see the cover of the Bible study you want to review. They are listed in alphabetical order. Choose the study by clicking on the cover image. On the next screen, select **Write a Review**. Write your review and **submit it**.

You can see our complete line of Bible studies, post a review, or order online and save at:

www.hensleypublishing.com

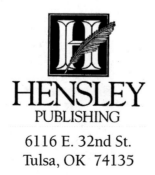

HENSLEY
PUBLISHING

6116 E. 32nd St.
Tulsa, OK 74135

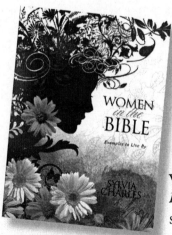